AF538002

# Preface

This text delivers a clear and developmental approach of Coordination Chemistry for B.Sc. and M.Sc. students of Inorganic Chemistry. The distinctive feature of the text is the acknowledgement that students learn and understand best when the arguments are progressively explained in detail, step-by-step. This is essentially important in this text where modern spectroscopy is a major component. This text provides detailed verbal clarification of the concepts and their importance to inorganic chemists. This text is scholarly, lucid and well written with a combination of depth of coverage and clarity. To understand the topics only basic school level mathematics is required.

**—Editor**

# CONTENTS

# 1

# INTRODUCTION

## What is a Coordination Compound?

*A coordination complex* is the product of a Lewis acid-base reaction in which neutral molecules or anions (called *ligands*) bond to a central metal atom (or ion) by *coordinate covalent bonds.*

(i) Ligands are Lewis bases—they contain at least one pair of electrons to donate to a metal atom/ion. Ligands are also called *complexing agents.*

(ii) Metal atoms/ions are Lewis acids—they can accept pairs of electrons from Lewis bases.

(iii) Within a ligand, the atom that is directly bonded to the metal atom/ion is called the *donor atom.*

(iv) A coordinate covalent bond is a covalent bond in which one atom (i.e., the donor atom) supplies both electrons. This type of bonding is different from a normal covalent bond in which each atom supplies one electron.

(v) If the coordination complex carries a net charge, the complex is called a *complex ion.*

(vi) Compounds that contain a coordination complex are called *coordination compounds.*

Coordination compounds and complexes are distinct chemical species-their properties and behaviour are different from the metal atom/ion and ligands from which they are composed.

The *coordination sphere* of a coordination compound or complex consists of the central metal atom/ion plus its attached ligands. The coordination sphere is usually enclosed in brackets when written in a formula.

The *coordination number* is the number of donor atoms bonded to the central metal atom/ion.

## Some Definitions

The transition metals are generally defined as the elements existing between the Alkali metals and earths (Groups 1 and 2) and the non-metal elements (Groups 13-18). That is they are the elements where the d-orbitals are being filled.

The first-row transition metals coincide with the filling of the 3-d orbitals and they are defined as possessing filled or partially filled valence d-orbitals in one or more of their oxidation states.

For this reason, Scandium and Zinc are usually ignored in simple discussions since Sc(III) and Zn(II) are their major oxidation states and these are $d^0$ and $d^{10}$ respectively.

A coordination compound, sometimes called a coordination complex, contains a central metal atom or ion surrounded by a number of oppositely charged ions or neutral molecules (possessing lone pairs of electrons) which are known as ligands.

If a ligand is capable of forming more than one bond with the central metal atom or ion, then ring structures are produced which are known as Metal Chelates, the ring forming groups are described as chelating agents or polydentate ligands.

The coordination number of the central metal atom or ion is the total number of sites occupied by ligands. Note: a bidentate ligand uses two sites, a tridentate three sites etc.

## Coordination Chemistry

Coordination chemistry is the study of compounds formed between metal ions and other neutral or negatively charged molecules such as $[Co(NH_2CH_2CH_2NH_2)_2ClNH_3]^{2+}$ $Cl_2^{2-}$. In this formulation, Co $(NH_2CH_2CH_2NH_2)_2ClNH_3]^{2+}$ is known as a metal complex, which is a charged species consisting of metal ion bonded to one or more groups of molecules. The bonded molecules are called ligand. The little picture shown here depicts a structure of a 6-coordinated complex.

A common metal complex is $Ag(NH_3)_2^+$, formed when $Ag^+$ ions are mixed with neutral ammonia molecules.

$Ag^+ + 2\ NH_3 \rightarrow Ag\ (NH_3)_2^+$

A complex Ag $(S_2O_3)_2^{3-}$ is formed between silver ions and negative thiosulphate ions:

$Ag^+ + 2\ S_2O_3^{2-} \rightarrow Ag(S_2O_3)_2^{3-}$

Metal complexes are also called **coordination compounds.** Their structures are important data and properties. Compounds having the same chemical formula but different structures are called **isomers**. Isomers with different geometic arrangements of ligands are called **geometric isomers** whereas isomers whose structures are mirror images of each other are called **optical isomers**. When a beam of polarised light passes optical isomers or their solutions, the plane or polarisation rotates in different directions. The beam rotates to the left for one isomer, and right for its mirror image.

## How did the study of coordination compounds started?

The coordination chemistry was pioneered by Nobel Prize winner Alfred Werner (1866-1919). He received the Nobel Prize in 1913 for his coordination theory of transition metal-amine complexes. At the start of the 20th century, inorganic chemistry was not a prominant field until Werner studied the metal-amine complexes such as [Co $(NH_3)_6Cl_3$].

Werner recognised the existence of several forms of cobalt-ammonia chioride. These compounds have different colour and other characteristics. The chemical formula has three chloride ions per mole, but the number of chloride ions that precipitate with $Ag^+$ ions per formula is not always three. He thought only ionized chloride ions will form precipitate with silver ion. In the following table, the number below the Ionized $Cl^-$ is the number of ionized chloride ions per formula. To distinguish ionized chloride from the coordinated chloride, Werner formulated the complex formula and explained structure of the cobalt complexes.

**Proposed Structure of Cobalt Amonia Complexes from Number of Ionized Chloride**

| Solid | Colour | Ionized Cl | Complex formula |
|---|---|---|---|
| $CoCl_3 6NH_3$ | Yellow | 3 | $[Co(NH_3)_6]Cl_3$ |
| $CoCl_3 5NH_3$ | Purple | 2 | $[Co(NH_3)_5Cl]Cl_2$ |
| $CoCl_3 4NH_3$ | Green | 1 | *trans*-$[Co(NH_3)_4Cl_2]$ Cl |
| $CoCl_3 4NH_3$ | Violet | 1 | *cis*-$[Co(NH_3)_4Cl_2]Cl$ |

The structures of the complexes were proposed based on a coordination sphere of 6. The 6 ligands can be amonia molecules or chloride ions. Two different structures were proposed for the last two compounds, the *trans* compound has two chioride ions on opposit vertices of an octahedral, whereas the two chloride ions are adjacent to each other in the *cis* compound. The *cis* and *trans* compounds are known as **geometric isomers**.

Other cobalt complexes studied by Werner are also interesting. It has been predicted that the complex $Co(NH_2CH_2CH_2NH_2)_2 ClNH_3]^{2+}$ should exist in two forms, which are mirror images of each other. Werner isolated solids of the two forms, and structural studies confirmed his interpretations. The ligand $NH_2CH_2CH_2NH_2$ is ethylenediamine (en) often represented by en.

## How are coordination compounds named?

Structures of coordination compounds can be very complicated, and their names long because the ligands may already have long names. Knowing the rules or nomenclature not only enable you to understand what the complex is, but also let you give appropriate names to them.

Often, several groups of the ligand are involved in a complex. The number of ligand molecules per complex is indicated by a Greek prefix: mono-, di- (or bis), tri-, tetra-, penta-, hexa, hepta, octa-, nona-, (ennea-), deca- etc for 1, 2, 3, ... 10 etc. If the names of ligands already have one of these prefixes, the names are placed in parentheses. The prefices for the number of ligands become bis-, tris-, tetrakis, pentakis-etc.

For neutral ligands, their names are not changed, except the following few:

$H_2O$, aqua

$NH_3$, ammine (not two m's, amine is for organic compounds)

CO, carbonyl

No, nitrosyl

Normal names that will not change

$C_5H_5N$, pyradine

$NH_2CH_2CH_2NH_2$, ethylenediamine

$C_5H_4N$-$C_5H_4N$, dipyridyl

$P(C_6H_5)_3$, triphenylphosphine

$NH_2CH_2CH_2NHCH_2CH_2NH_2$, diethylenetriamine

The last "e" in names of negative ions are changed to "o" in names of complexes. Sometimes "ide" is changed to "o". Note the following:

$Cl^-$, chloride -> chloro

$OH^-$, hydroxide -> hydroxo

$O^{2-}$, oxide -> oxo

$O_2^-$, peroxide, -> peroxo

$CN^-$, cyanide -> cyano

$N_3^-$, azide -> axido

$N^{3-}$, nitride -> nitrido

$NH_2^-$, amide -> amido

$CO_2^{2-}$, carbonate -> carbonate

-$ONO_2^-$, nitrate -> nitrato (when bonded through O)

-$NO_3^-$, nitrate -> nitro (when bonded through N)

$S^{2-}$, sulphide -> sulphido

$SCN^-$, thiocyanate -> thiocyanato-S

$NCS^-$, thiocyanate -> thiocyanato-N

-$(CH_2\text{-}N(CH_2COO^-)_2)_2$, ethylenediaminetetraacetato (EDTA)

The names of complexes start with the ligands, the anionic ones first, followed with neutral ligands and the metal. If the complex is negative, the name ends with "ate". At the very end are some Roman numerals representing the oxidation state of the metal.

To give and remember all rules of nomenclature are hard to do. Pay attention to the names whenever you encounter any complexes is the way to learn.

$[Co(NH_3)_5Cl]Cl_2$, Chloropentaamminecobalt (III) chloride

$[Cr(H_2O)_4Cl_2]Cl$, Dichlorotetraaquochromium (III) chloride

$K[PtCl_3NH_3]$, Potassiumtrichloroammineplatinate(II)

$PtCl_2(NH_3)_2$, Dichlorodiammineplatinum

$Co(en)_3Cl_3$, tris(ethylenediamine)cobalt(III)chloride

$Ni(PF_3)_4$, tetrakis(phosphorus(III)fluoride)nickel(0)

A bridgin ligand is indicated by placing a μ-before its name. The μ- should be repeated for every bridging ligand. For example, $(H_3N)_3Co(OH)_3Co(NH_3)_3$, Triamminecobalt(III)-μ-trihydroxotriamminecobalt(III)

*Example 1*

Give the structural formula for chlorotriphenylphosphinepalladium (II)-m-dichlorochlorotriphenylphosphinepalladium (II).

***Solution***

The structure is

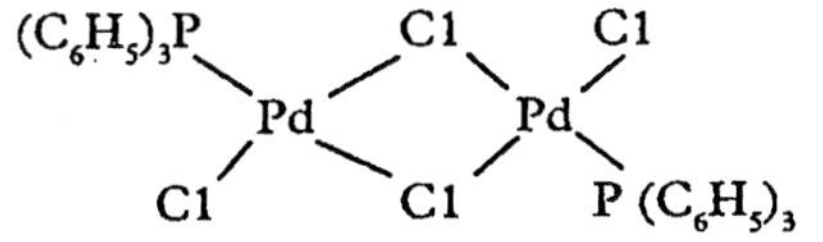

$$\begin{array}{ccccc} (C_6H_5)_3P & & Cl & & Cl \\ & Pd & & Pd & \\ Cl & & Cl & & P(C_6H_5)_3 \end{array}$$

***Discussion***

Answer the following questions:

- ⋆ How many ionized chloride ions are there per formula?
- ⋆ How many chloride ions act as bridges per formula in this complex?
- ⋆ How many types of chloride ligands are there in this complex?

***Exampe 2***

Name the complex:

$$(en)_2Co \overset{NH}{\underset{OH}{<\quad>}} Co\,(en)_2\,Cl_3$$

***Solution***

The name is Bis (ethylenediamine)cobalt(III)-μ-imido-μ-hydroxobis (ethylenediamine)cobalt(III) ion.

***Discussion***

When this compound dissolves in water, is the solution a conductor? What are the ions present in the solution of this compound? How many moles of chloride ions are present per mole of the compound?

When potassiumtrichloroammineplatinate(II)dissolves in water, what ions are produced? What about chloropentaamminecobalt (III) chloride?

# 2

# NOMENCLATURE OF COORDINATION COMPLEXES

## Introduction

Nomenclature is important in Coordination Chemistry because of the existence of isomers. In 1970, the International Union of Pure and Applied Chemistry (IUPAC), recommended changes to the existing 1957 rules of Inorganic Nomenclature. However, many tex books do not use these newer rules and should not be followed for guidance. For example, the 3rd Edition of "Basic Inorganic Chemistry" by F.A. Cotton, G. Wikinson and P.L. Gaus, John Wiley and Sons, Inc, 1995 page 181, is once again incorrect the 2nd Edition had it right!).

## The rules to follow are outlined below

1. In naming the entire complex, the name of the cation is given first and the anion second (just as for sodium chloride), no matter whether the cation or the anion is the complex species.

2. In the complex ion, the name of the ligand or ligands precedes that of the central metal atom. (This procedure is reversed for writing formulae.)

3. Ligand names generally end with 'o' if the ligand is negative ('chloro' for Cl-, 'cyano' for CN-, 'hydrido' for H-) and unmodified if the ligand is neutral ('methylamine' for $MeNH_2$). Special ligand names are 'aqua' for water, 'ammine' for ammonia 'carbonyl' for CO, 'nitrosyl' for NO.

4. A Greek prefix (mono, di, tri, tetra, penta, hexa, etc.) indicates the number of each ligand (mono is usually omitted for a single ligand of a given type). If the name of the ligand itself contains the terms mono, di, tri, eg triphenylphosphine, then the ligand name is enclosed in parentheses and its number is given with the alternate prefixes bis, tris, tetrakis instead.

For example, $Ni(PPh_3)_2Cl_2$ is named dichlorobis (triphenylphosphine)nickel(II).

To avoid the confusion as to whether "dimethylamine" means two separate methylamines or the single ligand dimethylamine, then for the former case it should be named as bis(methylamine). Some texts suggest that if a ligand is "complicated" then use the bis, tris multipliers. What constitutes "complicated" is not spelled out however, so a simpler approach is to use them if the name of the ligand is three or more syllables long.

5. A Roman numeral or a zero in parentheses is used to indicate the oxidation state of the central metal atom.

6. It the complex ion is negative, the name of the metal ends in 'ATE' for example, ferrate, cuprate, nickelate, cobaltate etc.

7. If more than one ligand is present in the species, then the ligands are named in alphabetical order regardless of the number of each. For example, $NH_3$ (ammine) would be considered an 'a' ligand and come before Cl- (chloro). (This is where the 1971 rules differ from the 1957 rules. Some texts still say that ligands are named in the order: neutral then anionic).

Some additional notes.

(i) Some metals in anions have special names

| | | | | | | | |
|---|---|---|---|---|---|---|---|
| B | Borate | Au | Aurate | Ag | Argentate | Fe | Ferrate |
| Pb | Plumbate | Sn | Stannate | Cu | Cuprate | | |

(ii) Use of brackets or enclosing marks.

Square brackets are used to enclose a complex ion or neutral coordination species. Examples:

$[Co(en)_3]Cl_3$

$[Co(NH_3)_3(NO_2)_3]$

$K_2[CoCl_4]$

note that it is not necessary to enclose the halogens in brackets.

# 3

# WERNER COMPLEXES

The history of modern coordination chemistry has been the subject of several books, of which perhaps the best known are those by George B. Kauffman. By necessity they all highlight Alfred Werner, "the Father of Coordination Chemistry" who in 1893, proposed the octahedral configuration of transition metal complexes and in 1913 received the first Nobel prize in Inorganic Chemistry.

In this series of experiments, some simple cobalt(III) complexes are to be prepared, which show some of the properties that Werner was able to interpret using the octahedral model. These include; opitcal, geometric and linkage isomerism.

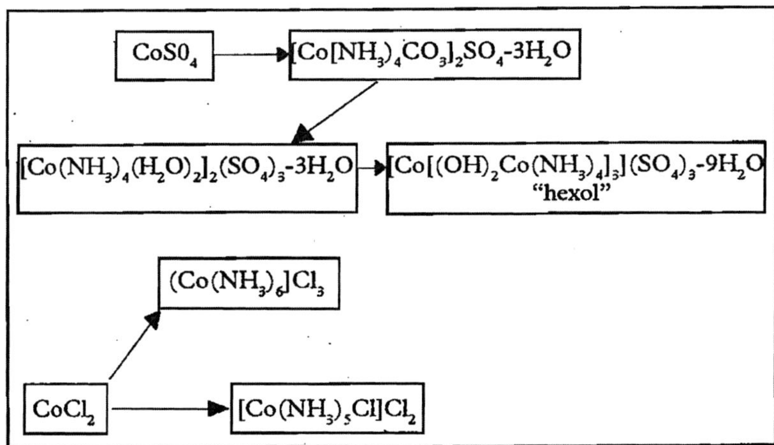


**Reaction Schemes as ISIS Draw .tgf file**

The oxidation of cobalt sulphate to the tetraamminecarbonate complex can be done by passing air through the solution for 2 hours, or more conveniently using hydrogen peroxide (although this is more costly, it allows the experiment to be easily completed in one session). The conversion of the bis-aqua complex to "hexol" given here is the method originally used by Jorgensen. By contrast, Werner added phridine to a hot, dilute acetic acid solution. "Hexol" exists in several hydrated forms, all of them dark purple-black crystals. Air-drying the crystals has been found to result in the ennea-hydrate, whereas drying at 98C or over sulphuric acid results in the tetrahydrate.

The nitrite ion ($NO_2^-$) is an example of an ambidentate ligand. That is, it can form a bond to a metal via either of two non-equivalent sites, from the N or from an O.

In the second scheme, two linkage isomers of the type $[Co(NH_3)_5ONO]^{2+}$ and $[Co(NH_3)_5NO_2]^{2+}$ are prepared starting from $[Co(NH_3)_5Cl]^{2+}$.

The actual isomer obtained depends on the pH of the solution. It should be noted that the two isomers are in equilibrium and that the nitro compound is the more stable. Whereas isomerisation takes several months at room temperature it is greatly accelerated by heating. Therefore the products should NOT be heated.

## Kinetic Study

The nitrito isomer converts slowly at room temperature to the nitro isomer and the conversion can be conveniently followed by observing the disappearance of the nitrito band at approximately 1060 $cm^{-1}$ in the IR spectrum.

Collect an IR spectrum of the penataamminechlorocobalt(III) chloride for comparison.

The kinetic study should be started as soon as the KBr pellet of the nitrito isomer has been prepared. The IR spectrum of this pellet is run between 1200 and 900 $cm^{-1}$ at various time intervals over a period of three weeks, ensuring that at least 6 recordings are made (e.g. 0, 0.125, 0.5, 2.0, 4.0, 11.0, 18.0 days).

The pellet should be kept in a dessicator in the dark at room temperature between readings.

It is assumed that for the KBr pellet the path length is constant; therefore the concentration of the complex is proportional to the Absorbance or log ($T_0/T$). The T value is read directly from the % transmittance recording paper and $T_0$ is estimated by connecting the baseline immediately to the left and right of the nitrito band and averaging the readings.

At the end of the experiment, the KBr pellet is placed in an oven at 100C to complete the isomerisation and to obtain an A (infinity) measurement. Plot a graph of log ($A-A_{inf}$) versus time. The rate constant k for isomerisation is equal to 2.303* slope and the reaction is found to obey first-order kinetics.

# 4

# COORDINATION COMPLEXES AND LIGANDS

## Coordination Complexes

Coordination compounds, such as the $FeCl_4^-$ ion and $CrCl_3 \cdot 6NH_3$, are called such because they contain ions or molecules linked, or coordinated, to a transition metal. They are also known as **complex ions** or **coordination complexes** because they are Lewis acid-base complexes. The ions or molecules that bind to transition-metal ions to form these complexes are called **ligands** (from Latin, "to tie or bind"). The number of ligands bound to the transition metal ion is called the **coordination number.**

Although coordination complexes are particularly important in the chemistry of the transition metals, some main group elements also form complexes. Aluminum, tin, and lead, for example, form complexes such as the $AlF_6^{3-}$, $SnCl_4^{2-}$ and $PbI_4^{2-}$ ions.

## Werner's Theory of Coordination Complexes

Alfred Werner developed a model of coordination complexes which explains the following observations.

* At least three different cobalt(III) complexes can be isolated when $CoCl_2$ is dissolved in aqueous ammonia and then oxidized by air to the +3 oxidation state. A fourth complex can be made by slightly different techniques. These complexes have different colours and different empirical formulae.

| | |
|---|---|
| $CoCl_2 . 6 NH_3$ | orange-yellow |
| $CoCl_3 . 5 NH_3 . H_2O$ | red |
| $CoCl_3 . 5 NH_3$ | purple |
| $CoCl_3 . 4 NH_3$ | green |

★ The reactivity of the ammonia in these complexes has been drastically reduced. By itself, ammonia reacts rapidly with hydrochloric acid to form ammonium chloride.

$$NH_3\ (aq) + HCl(aq) \rightarrow NH_4^+\ (aq) + Cl^-(aq)$$

These complexes don't react with hydrochloric acid, even at 100°C.

$$CoCl_3 . 6\ NH_3\ (aq) + HCl(aq) \rightarrow$$

★ Solutions of the $Cl^-$ ion react with $Ag^+$ ion to form a white precipitate of AgCl.

$$Ag^+(aq) + Cl^-(aq) \rightarrow AgCl(s)$$

When excess $Ag^+$ ion is added to solutions of the $CoCl_3 . 6 NH_3$ and $CoCl_3 . 5 NH_3 . H_2O$ complexes, three moles of AgCl are formed for each mole of complex in solution, as might be expected. However, only two of the $Cl^-$ ions in the $CoCl_3 . 5 NH_3$ complex and only one of the $Cl^-$ ions in $CoCl_3 . 4 NH_3$ can be precipitated with $Ag^+$ ions.

★ Measurements of the conductivity of aqueous solutions of these complexes suggest that the $CoCl_3 . 6 NH_3$ and $CoCl_3 . 5 NH_3 . H_2O$ complexes dissociate in water to give a total of four ions. $CoCl_3 . 5 NH_3$ dissociates to give three ions, and $CoCl_3 . 4NH_3$ dissociates to give only two ions.

Werner explained these observations by suggesting that transition-metal ions such as the $Co^{3+}$ ion have a primary valence and a secondary valence. The *primary valence* is the number of negative ions needed to satisfy the charge on the metal ior In each of the cobalt(III) complexes previously describe three $Cl^-$ ions are needeed to satisfy the primary valence of th $Co^{3+}$ ion.

The *secondary valence* is the number of ions of molecules that are coordinated to the metal ion. Werner assumed that the secondary valence of the transition metal in these cobalt(III) complexes is six. The formulae of these compunds can therefore be written as follows.

| | |
|---|---|
| $[Co(NH_3)_6{}^{3+}][Cl^-]_3$ | orange-yellow |
| $[Co(NH_3)_5(H_2O)^{3+}][Cl^-]_3$ | red |
| $[Co(NH_3)_5Cl^{2+}][Cl^-]_2$ | purple |
| $[Co(NH_3)_4Cl_2{}^+][Cl^-]$ | green |

The cobalt ion is coordinated to a total of six ligands in each complex, which satisfies the secondary valence of this ion. Each complex also has a total of three chloride ions that satisfy the primary valence. Some of the $Cl^-$ ions are free to dissociate when the complex dissolves in water. Others are bound to the $Co^{3+}$ ion and neither dissociate nor react with $Ag^+$.

The $[Co(NH_3)_6]Cl_3$ complex dissociates in water to give a total of four ions, and all three $Cl^-$ ions are free to react with $Ag^+$ ion.

$$[Co(NH_3)_6]Cl_3(s) \xrightarrow{H_2O} Co(NH_3)_6{}^{3+}(aq) + 3\ Cl^-(aq)$$

One of the chloride ions is bound to the cobalt in the $[Co(NH_3)_5Cl]Cl_2$ complex. Only three ions are formed when this compound dissolves in water, and only two $Cl^-$ ions are free to precipitate with $Ag^+$ ions.

$$[Co(NH_3)_5Cl][Cl]_2(s) \xrightarrow{H_2O} Co(NH_3)_5Cl^{2+}(aq) + 2\ Cl^-(aq)$$

One again, the three $Cl^-$ ions are free to dissociate when $[Co(NH_3)_5(H_2O)]Cl_3$ dissolves in water, and they precipitate when $Ag^+$ ions are added to the solution.

$$[Co(NH_3)_5(H_2O)]Cl_3(s) \xrightarrow{H_2O} Co(NH_3)_5(H_2O)^{3+}(aq)^{+3}\ Cl^-(aq)$$

Two of the chloride ions are bound to the cobalt in $[Co(NH_3)_4Cl_2]Cl$. Only two ions are formed when this compound dissolves in water, and only one $Cl^-$ ion is free to precipitate with $Ag^+$ ions.

$$[Co(NH_3)_4Cl_2][Cl](s) \xrightarrow{H_2O} Co(NH_3)_4Cl_2^{+}(aq) + Cl^{-}(aq)$$

Werner assumed that transition-metal complexes had definite shapes. According to his theory, the ligands in six-coordinate cobalt(III) complexes are oriented toward the corners of an octahedron, as shown in the figure below.

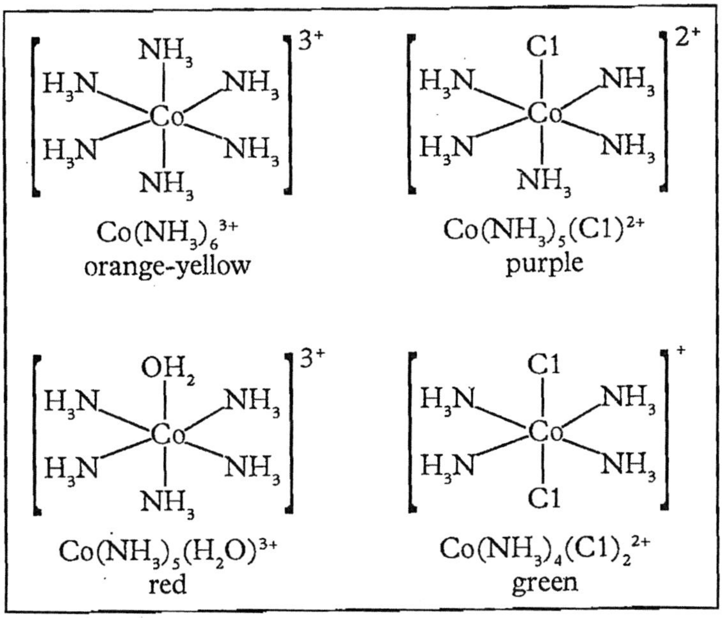

$Co(NH_3)_6^{3+}$
orange-yellow

$Co(NH_3)_5(Cl)^{2+}$
purple

$Co(NH_3)_5(H_2O)^{3+}$
red

$Co(NH_3)_4(Cl)_2^{2+}$
green

### *Typical Ligands*

Any ion or molecule with a pair of nonbonding electrons can be a ligand. Many ligands are described as monodentate (literally, "one-toothed") because they "bite" the metal in only one place. Typical monodentate ligands are given in the figure below.

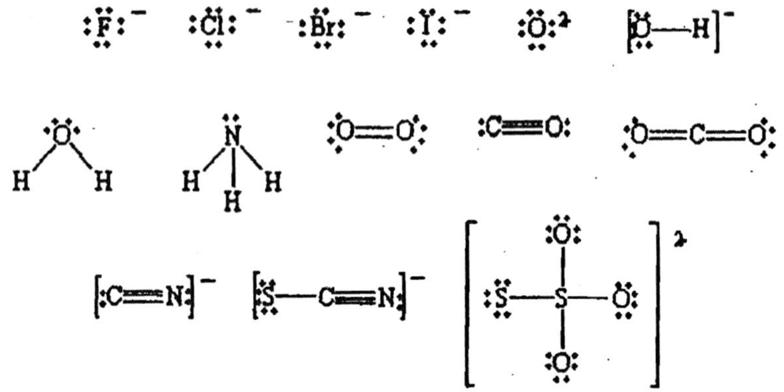

Other ligands can attach to the metal more than once. Ethylenediamine (en) is a typical bidentate ligand.

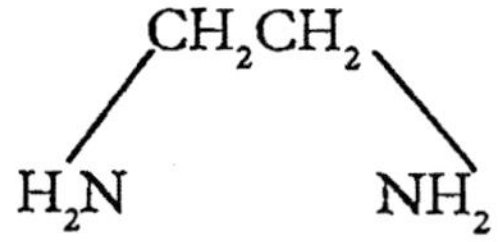

$CH_2CH_2$

$H_2N$ $NH_2$

ethylenediamine (en)

Each end of this molecule contains a pair of nonbonding electrons that can form a covalent bond to a metal ion. Ethylenediamine is also an example of a chelating ligand. The term *chelate* comes from a Greek stem meaning "claw." It is used to describe ligands that can grab the metal in two or more places, the way a claw would.

Linking ethylene-diamine fragments gives tridentate *ligands* and *tetradentate ligands,* such as diethylenetriamine (dien) and triethylenetetramine (trien). Adding four -$CH_2CO_2^-$ groups to an ethylenediamine framework gives a *hexadentate ligand,* which can single-handedly satisfy the secondary valence of a transition-metal ion.

**Tridentate Ligand:**

$H_2\ddot{N}-CH_2CH_2-\ddot{N}H-CH_2CH_2-\ddot{N}H$ diethylenetriamine (dien)

**Tetradentate Ligand:**

$H_2\ddot{N}-CH_2CH_2-\ddot{N}H-CH_2CH_2-\ddot{N}H-CH_2CH_2-\ddot{N}H$ triethylenetetraamine (trien)

**Hexadentate Ligand:**

$(^-{:}\ddot{O}-C(=O)CH_2)_2\ddot{N}CH_2CH_2\ddot{N}(CH_2C(=O)-\ddot{O}{:}^-)_2$ ethylenediaminetetraacetate (EDTA)

## *Typical Coordination Numbers*

Transition-metal complexes have been characterised with coordination numbers that range from 1 to 12, but the most common coordination numbers are 2, 4, and 6. Examples of complexes with these coordination numbers are given in the table below.

*Examples of Common Coordination Numbers*

| *Metal Ion* | | *Ligand* | | *Complex* | *Coordination Number* |
|---|---|---|---|---|---|
| $Ag^+$ | + | $2NH_3$ | $\rightleftharpoons$ | $Ag(NH_3)_2^+$ | 2 |
| $Ag^+$ | + | $2S_2O_3^{2-}$ | $\rightleftharpoons$ | $AgCl_2^-$ | 2 |
| $Ag^+$ | + | $2\ Cl^-$ | $\rightleftharpoons$ | $Ag(S_2O_3)_2^{3-}$ | 2 |
| $Pb^{2+}$ | + | $2\ OAc^-$ | $\rightleftharpoons$ | $Pb(OAc)_2$ | 2 |
| $Cu^+$ | + | $2\ NH_3$ | $\rightleftharpoons$ | $Cu(NH_3)_2^+$ | 2 |
| $Cu^{2+}$ | + | $4\ NH_3$ | $\rightleftharpoons$ | $Cu(NH_3)_4^{2+}$ | 4 |
| $Zn^{2+}$ | + | $4\ CN^-$ | $\rightleftharpoons$ | $Zn(CN)_4^{2-}$ | 4 |
| $Hg^{2+}$ | + | $4I^-$ | $\rightleftharpoons$ | $HgI_4^{2-}$ | 4 |
| $Co^{2+}$ | + | $4\ SCN^-$ | $\rightleftharpoons$ | $Co(SCN)_4^{2-}$ | 4 |

| | | | | | | |
|---|---|---|---|---|---|---|
| $Fe^{2+}$ | + | $6\ H_2O$ | $\rightleftharpoons$ | $Fe(H_2O)_6^{2+}$ | 6 |
| $Fe^{3+}$ | + | $6\ H_2O$ | $\rightleftharpoons$ | $Fe(H_2O)_6^{3+}$ | 6 |
| $Fe^{2+}$ | + | $6\ CN^-$ | $\rightleftharpoons$ | $Fe(CN)_6^{4-}$ | 6 |
| $Co^{3+}$ | + | $6\ NH_3$ | $\rightleftharpoons$ | $Co(NH_3)_6^{3+}$ | 6 |
| $Ni^{2+}$ | + | $6\ NH_3$ | $\rightleftharpoons$ | $Ni(NH_3)_6^{2+}$ | 6 |

Note that the charge on the complex is always the sum of the charges on the ions or molecules that form the complex.

$$Cu^{2+} + 4\,NH_3 \rightleftharpoons Cu(NH_3)_4^{2+}$$

$$Pb^{2+} + 2\,OAc^- \rightleftharpoons Pb(OAc)_2$$

$$Fe^{2+} + 6\,CN^- \rightleftharpoons Fe(CN)_6 4-$$

Note also that the coordination number of a complex often increases as the charge on the metal ion becomes larger.

$$Cu^{+} + 2\,NH_3 \rightleftharpoons Cu(NH_3)_2^{+}$$

$$Cu^{2+} + 4NH_3 \rightleftharpoons Cu(NH_3)_4^{2+}$$

*Lewis Acid-Lewis base Approach to Bonding in Complexes*

G.N. Lewis was the first to recognise that the reaction between a transition-metal ion and ligands to form a coordination complex was analogous to the reaction between the $H^+$ and $OH^-$ ions to form water. The reaction between $H^+$ and $OH^-$ ions involves the donation of a pair of electrons from the $OH^-$ ion to the $H^+$ ion to form a covalent bond.

$$H^+ \leftarrow O—H^- \rightarrow H—O—H$$

The $H^+$ ion can be described as an electron-pair acceptor. The $OH^-$ ion, on the other hand, is an electron-pair donor. Lewis argued that any ion or molecule that behaves like the $H^+$ ion should be an acid. Conversely, any ion or molecule that behaves like the $OH^-$ ion should be a base. A Lewis acid is therefore any ion or molecule that can accept a pair of electrons. A Lewis base is an ion or molecule that can donate a pair of electrons.

When $Co^{3+}$ ions react with ammonia, the $Co^{3+}$ ion accepts pairs of nonbonding electrons from six $NH_3$ ligands to form covalent cobalt-nitrogen bonds as shown in the figure below.

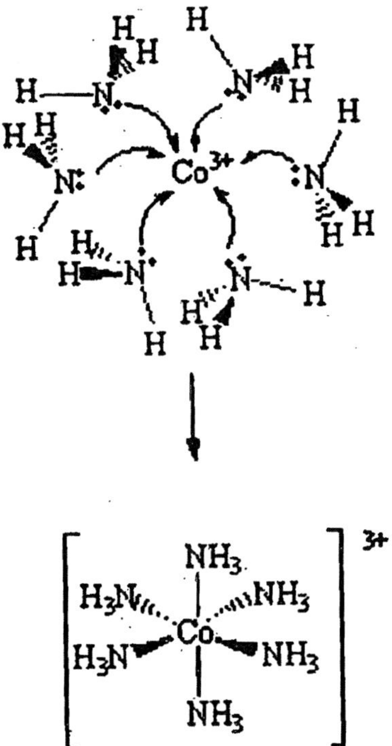


The metal ion is therefore a Lewis acid, and the ligands coordinated to this metal ion are Lewis bases.

| $Co^{3+}$ | + | $6NH_3$ | $\rightleftharpoons$ | $Co(NH_3)_3{}^{3+}$ |
|---|---|---|---|---|
| electron-pair acceptor (Lewis acid) | | electron-pair donor (Lewis base) | | acid-base complex |

The $Co^{3+}$ ion is an electron-pair acceptor, or Lewis acid, because it has empty valence-shell orbitals that can be used to hold pairs of elctrons. To emphasise these empty valence orbitals we can write the configuration of the $Co^{3+}$ ion as follows.

$$Co^{3+}\text{: [Ar] } 3d^6\ 4s^0\ 4p^0$$

There is room in the valence shell of this ion for 12 more electrons. (Four electrons can be added to the 3*d* subshell, two to the 4*s* orbital, and six to the 4*p* subshell.) The $NH_3$ molecule is an electron-pair donor, or Lewis base, because it has a pair of nonbonding electrons on the nitrogen atom.

According to this model, transition-metal ions form coordination complexes because they have empty valence-shell orbitals that can accept pairs of electrons from a Lewis base. Ligands must therefore be Lewis bases: They must contain at least one pair of nonbonding electrons that can be donated to a metal ion.

# 5

# STABILITY, CHELATION AND THE CHELATE EFFECT

## Introduction

A metal ion in solution does not exist in isolation, but in combination with ligands (such as solvent molecules or simple ions) or chelating groups, giving rise to complex ions or coordination compounds.

These complexes contain a central atom or ion, often a transition metal, and a cluster of ions or neutral molecules surrounding it. Many complexes are relatively unreactive species remaining unchanged throughout a sequence of chemical or physical operations and can often be isolated as stable solids or liquid compounds.

Other complexes have a much more transient existence and may exist only in solution or be highly reactive and easily converted to other species.

All metals from complexes, although the extent of formation and nature of these depend very largely on the electronic structure of the metal.

The concept of a metal complex originated in the work of Alfred Werner, who in 1913 was awarded the first Nobel Prize in Inorganic chemistry. A description of his life and the influence his work played in the development of coordination chemistry is given by G.B. Kauffman in "*Inorganic Coordination Compounds*", Heyden & Son Ltd. 1981.

Complexes may be non-ionic (neutral) or cationic or anionic, depending on the charges carried by the central metal ion and the coordinated groups. The total number of points of attachment to the central element is termed the coordination number and this can vary from 2 to greater than 12, but is usually 6.

The term **ligand** (**ligare [Latin], to bind**) was first used by Alfred Stock in 1916 in relation to silicon chemistry. The first use of the term in a British journal was by H. Irving and R.J.P. Williams in *Nature,* 1948, 162, 746.

For a fascinating review of the origin and dissemination of the term 'ligand' in chemistry see: W.H. Brock, K.A. Jensen, C.K. Jorgensen and G.B. Kauffman, *Polyhedron,* 2, 1983, 1-7.

Ligands can be further characterised as monodentate, bidentate, tridentate etc. where the concept of teeth (dent) is introduced, hence the idea of bite angle etc.

The term **chelate** was first applied in 1920 by Sir Gilbert T. Morgan and H.D.K. Drew [*J. Chem.Soc.*, 1920, 117, 1456], who stated:

"The adjective chelate, derived from the great claw or **chela (chely-Greek)** of the lobster or other crustaceans, is suggested for the caliperlike groups which function as two associating units and fasten to the central atom so as to produce heterocyclic rings."

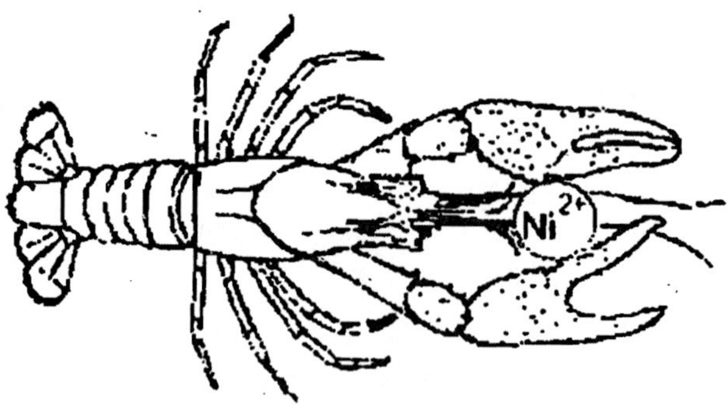


Metal complexation is of widespread interest. It is studied not only by inorganic chemists, but by physical and organic chemists and by biochemists, pharmacologists, molecular biologists and environmentalists.

## Thermodynamic Stability

In the liboratory course, it will have been pointed out that the "stability of a complex in solution" refers to the degree of association between the two species involved in the state of equilibrium. Qualitatively, the greater the association, the greater the stability of the compound. The magnitude of the (stability or formation) equilibrium constant for the association, quantitatively expresses the stability. Thus, if we have a reaction of the type:

$M + 4L \rightarrow ML_4$

then the larger the stability constant, the higher the proportion of $ML_4$ that exists in the solution. Free metal ions rarely exist in solution so that M, will usually be surrounded by solvent molecules which will complete with the ligand molecules, L, and be successively replaced by them. For simplicity, we generally ignore these solvent molecules and write four stability constants as follows:

1. $M + L \rightarrow ML$ $\quad K_1 = [ML]/[M][L]$
2. $ML + L \rightarrow ML_2$ $\quad K_2 = [ML_2]/[ML][L]$
3. $ML_2 + L \rightarrow ML_3$ $\quad K_3 = [ML_3]/[ML_2][L]$
4. $ML_3 + L \rightarrow ML_4$ $\quad K_4 = [ML_4]/[ML_3][L]$

where $K_1$, $K_2$ etc. are referred to as "stepwise stability constants".

Alternatively, we can write the "Overall Stability Constant" thus:

$M + 4L \rightarrow ML_4 \quad \beta_4 = [ML_4]/[M][L]^4$

The stepwise and overall stability constants are therefore related as follows:

$\beta_4 = K_1.K_2.K_3.K_4$ or more generally,

$\beta_n = K_1.K_2.K_3.K_4$------------$K_n$

If we take as an example, the steps involved in the formation of the cuprammonium ion, we have the following:

$Cu^{2+} + NH_3 \leftrightarrow [Cu(NH_3)^{2+}] \quad K1 = [Cu(NH_3)^{2+}]/[Cu^{2+}][NH_3]$

$CuNH_3^{2+} + NH_3 \leftrightarrow Cu(NH_3)_2^{2+} \quad K2 = [Cu(NH_3)_2^{2+}]/[Cu(NH_3)^{2+}][NH_3]$

etc. where $K_1$, $K_2$ are the stepwise stability constants

Also:

$$\beta_4 = [Cu(NH_3)_4{}^{2+}]/[Cu^{2+}]\,[NH_3]4$$

The addition of the four ammine groups to copper shows a pattern found for most formation constants, in that the successive stability constants decrease. In this case, the four constants are:

$\log K_1 = 4.0$, $\log K_2 = 3.2$, $\log K_3 = 2.7$, $\log K_4 = 2.0$ or $\log\beta_4 = 11.9$

A number of texts refer to the **instability constant or the dissociation constant** of coordination complexes. This value corresponds to the reciprocal of the formation constant, since the reactions referred to are those where fully formed complexes break to the aqua ion and free ligands. This should be compared with the equation for the formation constant given earlier.

So, it is usual to represent the metal-binding process by a series of stepwise equilibria which lead to stability constants that may vary numerically from hundreds to enormous values such as $10^{35}$ and more. For this reason, they are commonly reported as logarithms. It is additionally useful to use logarithms, since log(K) is directly proportional to the free energy of the reaction.

$$\Delta G^\circ = -RT\mathrm{Ln}\beta$$

$$\Delta G^\circ = -\ 2.303\ RT\mathrm{Log}_{10}\beta$$

$$\Delta G^\circ = \Delta H^\circ - T\Delta S^\circ$$

For a problem relating to metal complex formation and calculations of free metal ions concentrations, try your hand at CALCULATION # ONE Other problems can be found in the Tutorial paper for this course.

## The Chelate Effect

The chelate effect can be seen by comparing the reaction of a chelating ligand and a metal ion with the corresponding reaction involving comparable monodentate ligands. For example, comparison of the binding of 2,2'- bipyridine with pyridine or 1,2- diaminoethane (ethylenediamine=en) with ammonia.

It has been known for many years that a comparison of this type always shows that the complex resulting from coordination with the chelating ligand is much more thermodynamically stable. This can be seen by looking at the values for adding two monodentates compared with adding one bidentate, or adding four monodentates compared to two bidentates, or adding six monodentates compared to three bidentates.

## Some tables of thermodynamic data

Reaction of ammonia and 1,2 diaminoethane with $Cd^{2+}$.

| #of ligands | ΔG° ($kJmol^{-1}$) | ΔH° ($kJmol^{-1}$) | ΔS° ($JK^{-1}mol^{-1}$) | logβ |
|---|---|---|---|---|
| 2 $NH_3$ | -28.24 | -29.79 | -5.19 | 4.95 |
| (1 en) | (-33.30) | (-29.41) | (+13.05) | (5.84) |
| 4 $NH_3$ | -42.51 | -53.14 | -35.50 | 7.44 |
| (2 en) | (-60.67) | (-56.48) | (+13.15) | 10.62) |

Reaction of pyridine and 2,2′-bipyridine with $Ni^{2+}$.

| # of ligands | logβ | ΔG° ($kJmol^{-1}$) |
|---|---|---|
| 2 py (1 bipy) | 3.5 (6.9) | -20 (-39) |
| 4 py (2 bipy) | 5.6 (13.6) | -32.(-78) |
| 6 py (3 bipy) | 9.8 (19.3) | -56 (-110) |

Reaction of ammonia and 1,2-diaminoethane with $Ni^{2+}$.

| # of ligands | log β | ΔG° ($kJmol^{-1}$) |
|---|---|---|
| 1 $NH_3$ | 2.8 | -16 |
| 2 $NH_3$ (1 en) | 5.0 (7.51) | -28.5 (-42.8) |
| 3 $NH_3$ | 6.6 | -37.7 |
| 4$NH_3$ (2 en) | 7.87 (13.86) | -44.9 (-79.1) |
| 5 $NH_3$ | 8.6 | -49.1 |
| 6 $NH_3$ (3 en) | 8.61 (18.28) | -49.2 (-104.4) |

A number of points should be highlighted from this data.

In the first table, it can be seen that the ΔH° values for the formation steps are almost identical, that is, heat is evolved to about the same extent whether forming a complex involving monodentate ligands or bidentate ligands.

What is seen to vary significantly is the ΔS° term which changes from negative (unfavourable) to positive (favourable). Note as well that there is a dramatic increase in the size of the ΔS° term for adding two compared to adding four monodentate ligands. (-5 to -35 $JK^{-1} mol^{-1}$).

What does this imply, if we consider ΔS° to give a measure of disorder?

In the case of complex formation of $Ni^{2+}$ with ammonia or 1,2-diaminoethane, by rewriting the equilibria, the following equation are produced.

| | | | | |
|---|---|---|---|---|
| | | $\beta_6$ | | |
| $[Ni(H_2O)]^{2+}$ | $+ 6 NH_3$ | $\Leftrightarrow$ | $[Ni(NH_3)_6]^{2+}$ | 1f |
| $[Ni(NH_3)_6]^{2+}$ | | $\Leftrightarrow$ | $[Ni(H_2O)_6]^{2+} + 6 NH_3$ | 1d |
| | | β3 | | |
| $[Ni(H_2O)_6]^{2+}$ | $+ 3$ en | $\Leftrightarrow$ | $[Ni(en)_3]^{2+}$ | 2f |
| $[Ni(NH_3)_6]^{2+}$ | $+ 3$ en | $\Leftrightarrow$ | $[Ni(en)_3]^{2+} + 6NH_3$ | 3 |

Using the equilibrium constant for the reaction (3 above) where the three bidentates replace the six monodentates, we find that at a temperature of 25C:

$$\Delta G^\circ = -2.303\ RT \log_{10} (K)$$
$$= -2.303\ RT\ (18.28 - 8.61)$$
$$= -54 kj\ mol^{-1}$$

Based on measurements made over a range of temperatures, it is possible to break down the ΔG° term into the enthalpy and entropy components. The result is that:

$$\Delta H^\circ = -29\ kJ\ mol^{-1}$$

$-T\Delta S^o = -25$ kJ $mol^{-1}$
and at 25C (298K)
$\Delta S^o = +88$ $JK^{-1}$ $mol^{-1}$

Note that for many years, these numbers have been ncorrectly recorded in textbooks. For example, the third edition of "Basic Inorganic Chemistry" by F.A. Cotton, G. Wilkinson and P.L. Gaus, John Wiley & Sons, Inc, 1995, gives the values as:

$\Delta G^o = -67$ kJ $mol^{-1}$
$\Delta H^o = -12$ kJ $mol^{-1}$
$-T\Delta S^o = -55$ kJ $mol^{-1}$

The conclusion they drew from these incorrect numbers was that the chelate effect was essentially an entropy effect, since the $T\Delta S^o$ contribution was nearly 5 times bigger than $\Delta H^o$.

In fact, the breakdown of the $\Delta G^o$ into $\Delta H^o$ and $T\Delta S^o$ shows that the two terms are nearly equal with the $\Delta H^o$ term just slightly bigger! The entropy term found is still much larger than for reactions involving non-chelating ligand substitution at a metal ion.

How can we explain this enhanced contribution from entropy? One explanation is to count the number of species on the left and right hand side of the equation above.

It will be seen that on the left-hand-side there are 4 species, whereas on the right-hand-side there are 7 species, that is a net gain of 3 species occurs as the reaction proceeds. This can account for the increase in entropy since it represents an increase in the disorder of the system.

An alternative view comes from trying to understand how the reactions might proceed. To form a complex with 6 monodentates requires 6 separate favourable collisions between the metal ion and the ligand molecules. To form the tris-bidentate metal complex requires an initial collision for the first ligand to attach by one arm but remember that the other arm is always going to be nearby and only requires a rotation of the other end to enable the ligand to form the chelate ring.

If you consider dissociation steps, then when a monodentate group is displaced, it is lost into the bulk of the solution. On the other hand, if one end of a bidentate group is displaced the other arm is still attached and it is only a matter of the arm rotating around and it can be reattached again.

Both sets of conditons favour the formation of the complex with bidentate groups rather than monodentate groups.

# 6

# THE VALENCE-BOND APPROACH TO BONDING IN COMPLEXES

The idea that atoms form covalent bonds by sharing pairs of electrons was first proposed by G.N. Lewis in 1902. It was not until 1927, however, that Walter Heitler and Fritz London showed how the sharing of pairs of electrons holds a covalent molecule together. The Heitler-London model of covalent bonds was the basis of the valence-bond theory. The last major step in the evolution of this theory was the suggestion by Linus Pauling that atomic orbitals mix to form hybrid orbitals, such as the $sp$, $sp^2$, $sp^3$, $dsp^3$, and $d^2sp^3$ orbitals.

It is easy to apply the valence-bond theory to some coordination complexes, such as the $Co(NH_3)_6^{3+}$ ion. We start with the electron configuration of the transition-metal ion.

$$Co^{3+}: [Ar]\ 3d^6$$

We then look at the valence-shell orbitals and note that the 4*s* and 4*p* orbitals are empty.

$$Co^{3+}: [Ar]\ 3d^6\ 4s^0\ 4p^0$$

Concentrating the 3*d* electrons in the $d_{xy}$, $d_{xz}$, and $d_{yz}$ orbitals in this subshell gives the following electron configuration.

$$Co^{3+}: \underline{\uparrow\downarrow}\ \underline{\uparrow\downarrow}\ \underline{\uparrow\downarrow}\ \underline{\quad}\ \underline{\quad}\quad \underline{\quad}\quad \underline{\quad}\ \underline{\quad}\ \underline{\quad}$$

*3d*          *4s*          *4p*

The $3d_{x^2-y^2}$, $3d_{z^2}$, 4s, $4p_x$, $4p_y$ and $4p_z$ orbitals are then mixed to form a set of empty $d^2sp^3$ orbitals that point toward the corners of an octahedron. Each of these orbitals can accept a pair of nonbonding electrons from a neutral $NH_3$ molecule to form a complex in which the cobalt atom has a filled shell of valence electrons.

$Co(NH_3)_6^{3+}$ ⥮ ⥮ ⥮ ⥮ ⥮ ⥮ ⥮ ⥮ ⥮
3d 4s 4p

At first glance, complexes such as the $Ni(NH_3)_6^{2+}$ ion seem hard to explain with the valence-bond theory. We start, as always, by writing the configuration of the transition-metal ion.

$Ni^{2+}$: [Ar] $3d^8$

This configuration creates a problem, because there are eight electrons in the 3*d* orbitals. Even if we invest the energy necessary to pair the 3*d* electrons, we can't find two empty 3*d* orbitals to use to form a set of $d^2sp^3$ hybrids.

$Ni^{2+}$: ⥮ ⥮ ⥮ ⥮ _ _ _ _ _
3d 4s 4p

There is a way around this problem. The five 4*d* orbitals on nickel are empty, so we can form a set of empty $sp^3d^2$ hybrid orbitals by mixing the $4d_{x^2-y^2}$, $4d_{z^2}$, 4*s*, $4p_x$, $4p_y$ and $4p_z$ orbitals. These hybrid orbitals then accept pairs of nonbonding electrons from six ammonia molecules to form a complex ion.

$Ni(NH_3)_6^{2+}$ ⥮ ⥮ ⥮ ⥮ _ ⥮ ⥮ ⥮ ⥮ ⥮ ⥮ _ _ _
3d 4s 4p 4d

The valence-bond theory therefore formally distinguishes between "inner-shell" complexes, whch use 3*d*, 4*s* and 4*p* orbitals to form a set of $d^2sp^3$ hybrids, and outer-shell" complexes, which use 4*s*, 4*p* and 4*d* orbitals to form $sp^3d^2$ hybrid orbitals.

# 7

# CRYSTAL FIELD THEORY

At almost exactly the same time that chemists were developing the valence-bond model for coordination complexes, physicists such as Hans Bethe, John Van Vleck, and Leslie Orgel were developing an alternative known as **crystal field theory.** This theory tried to describe the effect of the electrical field of neighbouring ions on the energies of the valence orbitals of an ion in a crystal. Crystal field theory was developed by considering two compounds: manganese(II) oxide, MnO, and copper(I) chloride, CuCl.

## Octahedral Crystal Fields

Each $Mn^{2+}$ ion in manganese(II) oxide is surrounded by six $O^{2-}$ ions arranged toward the corners of an octahedron, as shown in the figure below. MnO is therefore a model for an *octahedral* complex in which a transition-metal ion is coordinated to six ligands.

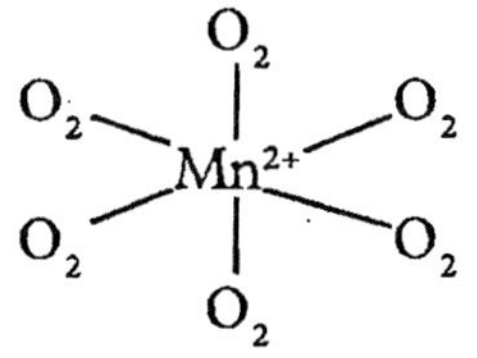

$O_2$
$O_2$ $O_2$
$Mn^{2+}$
$O_2$ $O_2$
$O_2$

What happens to the energies of the 4*s* and 4*p* orbitals on an $Mn^{2+}$ ion when this ion is buried in an MnO crystal? Repulsion between electrons that might be added to these orbitals and the electrons on the six $O^{2-}$ ions that surround the metal ion in MnO increase the energies of these orbitals. The three 4*p* orbitals are still degenerate, however. These orbitals still have the same energy because each 4*p* orbital points toward two $O^{2-}$ ions at the corners of the octahedron.

Repulsion between electrons on the $O^{2-}$ ions and electrons in the 3*d* orbitals on the metal ion in MnO also increases the energy of these orbitals. BUt the five 3*d* orbitals on the $Mn^{2+}$ ion are no longer degenerate. Let's assume that the six $O^{2-}$ ions that surround each $Mn^{2+}$ ion define an *XYZ* coordinate system. Two of the 3*d* orbitals ($3d_{x^2-y^2}$ and $3d_{z^2}$) on the $Mn^{2+}$ ion point directly toward the six $O^{2-}$ ions, as shown in the figure below. The other three orbitals ($3d_{xy}$, $3d_{xz}$ and $3d_{yz}$) lie between the $O^{2-}$ ions.

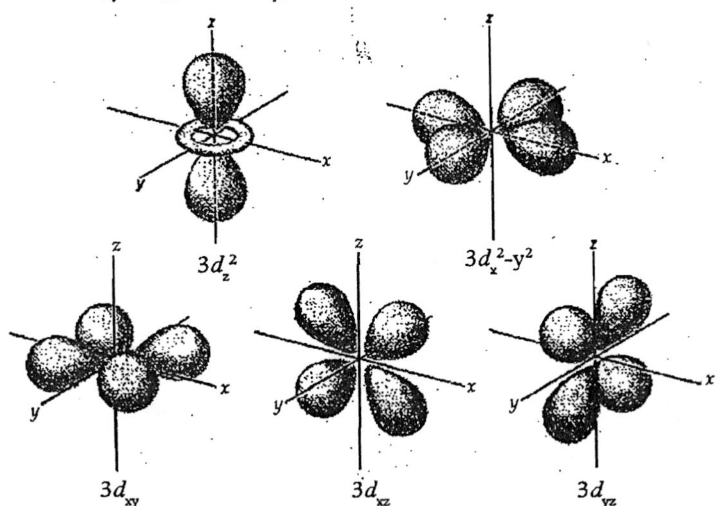


The energy of the five 3*d* orbitals increases when the six $O^{2-}$ ions are brought close to the $Mn^{2+}$ ion. However, the energy of two of these orbitals ($3d_{x^2-y^2}$ and $3d_{z^2}$) increases much more than the energy of the other three ($3d_{xy}$, $3d_{xz}$, and $3d_{yz}$) as shown in the figure below. The crystal field of the six $O^{2-}$ ions in MnO therefore splits the degeneracy of the five 3*d* orbitals. Three of these orbitals are now lower in energy than the other two.

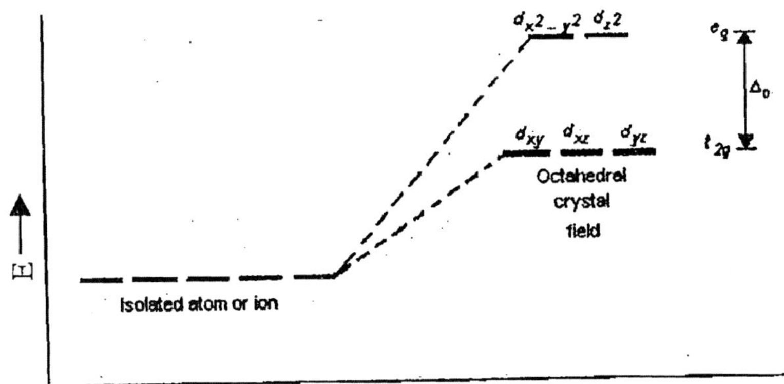


By convention, the $d_{xy}$, $d_{xz}$, and $d_{yz}$ orbitals in an octahedral complex are called the $t_{2g}$ orbitals. The $d_{x^2-y^2}$ and $d_{z^2}$ orbitals, on the other hand, are called the $e_g$ orbitals.

The easiest way to remember this convention is to note that there are three orbitals in the $t_{2g}$ set.

$$t_{2g}:\ d_{xy}, d_{xz}, \text{and } d_{yz} \quad e_g:\ d_{x^2-y^2} \text{ and } d_{z^2}$$

The difference between the energies of the $t_{2g}$ and $e_g$ orbitals in an octahedral complex is represented by the symbol $\Delta_o$. This splitting of the energy of the *d* orbitals is not trival; $\Delta_o$ for the $Ti(H_2O)_6^{3+}$ ion, for example, is 242 kJ/mol.

The magnitude of the splitting of the $t_{2g}$ and $e_g$ orbitals changes from one octahedral complex to another. It depends on the identity of the metal ion, the charge on this ion, and the nature of the ligands coordinated to the metal ion.

## Tetrahedral Crystal Fields

Each $Cu^+$ ions in copper(I) chloride is surrounded by four $Cl^-$ ions arranged toward the corners of a tetahendron, as shown in the figure below. CuCl is therefore a model for a *tetrahedral* complex in which a transition-metal ion is coordinated to four ligands.

$Cl^-$
|
$Cu^+$ — $Cl^-$
$Cl^-$ $Cl^-$

Once again, the negative ions in the crystal split the energy of the *d* atomic orbitals on the transition-metal ion. The tetrahendral crystal field splits these orbitals into the same $t_{2g}$ and $e_g$ sets of orbitals as does the octahedral crystal field.

$t_{2g}$: $d_{xy}$, $d_{xz}$, and $d_{yz}$ eg: $d_{x^2-y^2}$ and $d_{z^2}$

But the two orbitals in the $e_g$ set are now lower in energy than the three orbitals in the $t_{2g}$ set, as shown in the figure below.

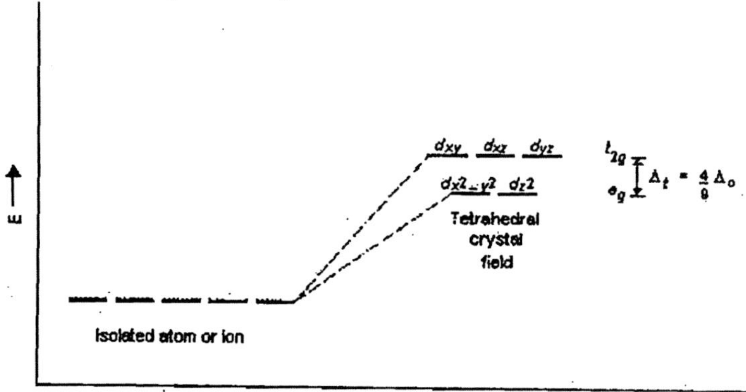


To understand the splitting of *d* orbitals in a tetrahedral crystal field, imagine four ligands lying at alternating corners of a cube to form a tetrahedral geometry, as shown in the figure below. The $d_{x^2-y^2}$ and $d_{z^2}$ orbitals on the metal ion at the centre of the cube lie between the ligands, and the $d_{xy}$, $d_{xz}$, and $d_{yz}$ orbitals points toward the ligands. As a result, the splitting observed in a tetrahedral crystal field is the opposite of the splitting in an octahedral complex.

Because a tetrahedral complex has fewer ligands, the magnitude of the splitting is smaller. The difference between the energies of the $t_{2g}$ and $e_g$ orbitals in a tetrahedral complex ($\Delta_t$) is slightly less than half as large as the splitting in analogous octahedral complexes ($\Delta_o$).

$$\Delta_t = {}^4/_9\ \Delta_o$$

## Square-Planar Complexes

The crystal field theory can be extended to square-planar complexes, such as $Pt(NH_3)_2Cl_2$. The splitting of the *d* orbitals in these compounds is shown in the figure on next page.

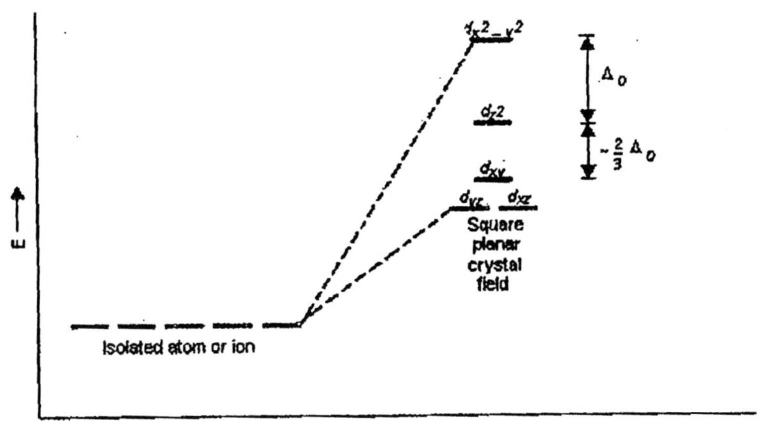


## The Spectrochemical Series

The splitting of *d* orbitals in the crystal filed model not only depends on the geometry of the complex, it also depends on the nature of the metal ion, the charge on this ion, and the ligands that surround the metal. When the geometry and the ligands are held constant, this splitting decreases in the following order.

$Pt^{4+} > Ir^{3+} > Rh^{3+} > Co^{3+} > Cr^{3+} > Fe^{3+} > Fe^{2+} > Co^{2+} > Ni^{2+} > Mn^{2+}$

strong-field ligands weak-field ligands

Metal ions at one end of this continuum are called *strong-field ions,* because the splitting due to the crystal field is unusually strong. Ions at the other end are known as *weak-field ions.*

When the geometry and the metal are held constant, the splitting of the *d* orbitals decreases in the following order.

$CO\ CN^- > NO_2^- > NH_3 > -NCS^- > H_2O > OH^-\ F^-\ -SCN^-\ Cl^- > Br^-$

strong-field ligands weak-field ligands

Ligands that give rise to large differences between the energies of the $t_{2g}$ and $e_g$ orbitals are called *strong-field ligands.* Those at the opposite extreme are known as *weak-field ligands.*

Because they result from studies of the absorption spectra of transition-metal complexes, these generalisations are known as the spectrochemical series. The range of values of Δ for a given geometry is remarkably large. The value of $\Delta_o$ is 100 kJ/mol in the $Ni(H_2O)_6^{2+}$ ion, for example, and 520 kJ/mol in the $Rh(CN)_6^{3-}$ ion.

## High-Spin Versus Low-Spin Octahedral Complexes

Once we know the relative energies of the *d* orbitals in a transition-metal complex, we have to worry about how these orbitals are filled. Degenerate orbitals are filled according to Hund's rules.

- ★ One electron is added to each of the degenerate orbitals in a subshell before a second electron is added to any orbital in the subshell.
- ★ Electrons are added to a subshell with the same value of the spin quantum number until each orbital in the subshell has at least one electron.

Octahedral transition-metal ions with $d^1$, $d^2$, or $d^3$ configurations can therefore be described by the following diagrams.

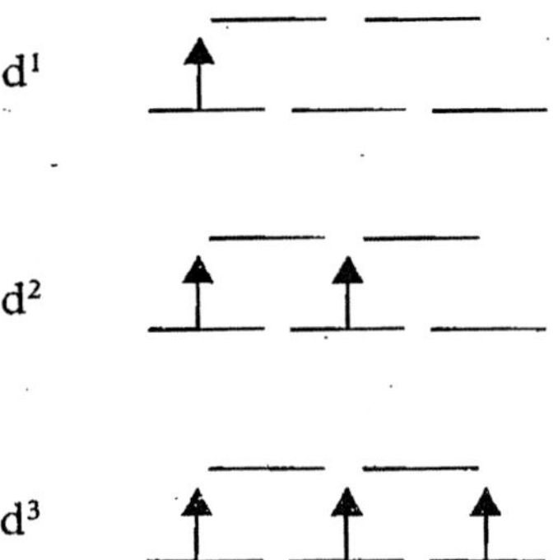


When we try to add a fourth electron, we are faced with a problem. This electron could be used to pair one of the electrons in the lower energy ($t_{2g}$) set of orbitals or it could be placed in one of the higher energy ($e_g$)orbitals. One of these configurations is called **high-spin** because it contains four unpaired electrons with the same spin. The other is called **low-spin** because it contains only two unpaired electrons. The same problem occurs with octahedral $d^5$, $d^6$, and $d^7$ complexes.

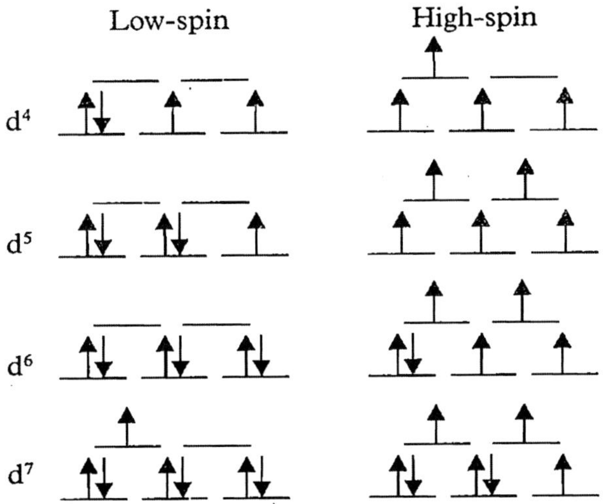


For octahedral $d^8$, $d^9$, and $d^{10}$ complexes, there is only one way to write satisfactory configurations.

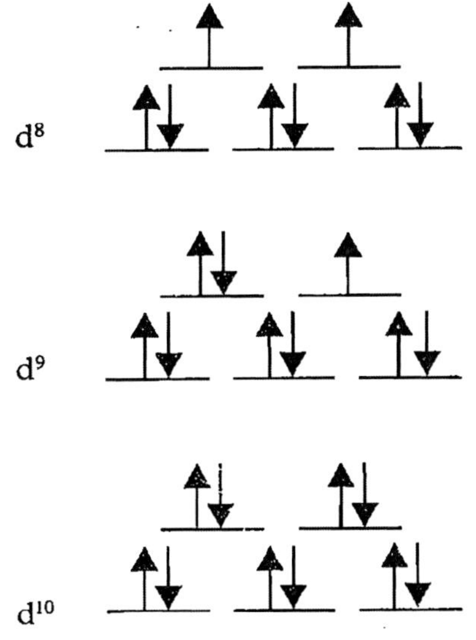

As a result, we have to worry about high-spin versus low-spin octahedral complexes only when there are four, five, six, or seven electrons in the *d* orbitals.

The choice between high-spin and low-spin configurations for octahedral $d^4$, $d^5$, $d^6$, or $d^7$ complexes is easy. All we have to do is compare the energy it takes to pair electrons with the energy it takes to excite an electron to the higher energy ($e_g$) orbitals. If it takes less energy to pair the electrons, the complex is low-spin. If it takes less energy to excite the electron, the complex is high-spin.

The amount to energy required to pair electrons in the $t_{2g}$ orbitals of an octahedral complex is more or less constant. The amount of energy needed to excite an electron into the higher energy ($e_g$) orbitals, however, depends on the value of $\Delta_o$ for the complex. As a result, we expect to find low-spin complexes among metal ions and ligands that lie toward the high-field end of the spectrochemical series. High-spin complexes are expected among metal ions and ligands that lie toward the low-field end of those series.

Compounds in which all of the electrons are paired are diamagnetic—they are repelled by both poles of a magnet. Compounds that contain one or more unpaired electrons are paramagnetic—they are attracted to the poles of a magnet. The force of attraction between paramagnetic complexes and a magnetic field is proportional to the number of unpaired electrons

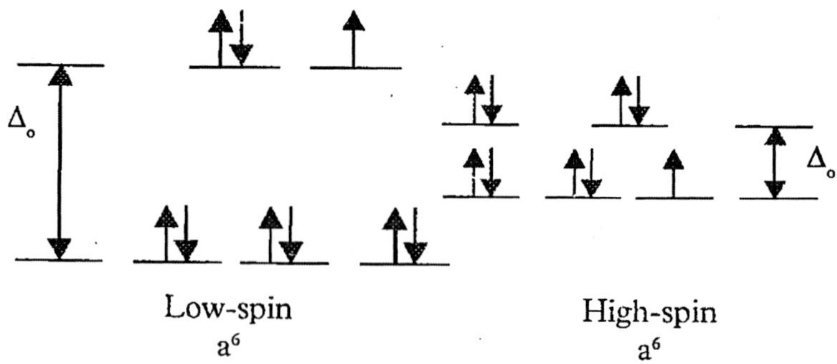

in the complex. We can therefore determine whether a complex is high-spin or low-spin by measuring the strength of the interaction between the complex and a magnetic field.

# 8

# LIGAND-FIELD THEORY

The *valence-bond model* and the *crystal field theory* explain some aspects of the chemistry of the transition metals, but neither model is good at predicting all of the properties of transition-metal complexes. A third model, based on molecular orbital theory, was therefore developed that is known as **ligand-field theory**. Ligand-field theory is more powerful than either the valence-bond or crystal-field theories. Unfortunately it is also more abstract.

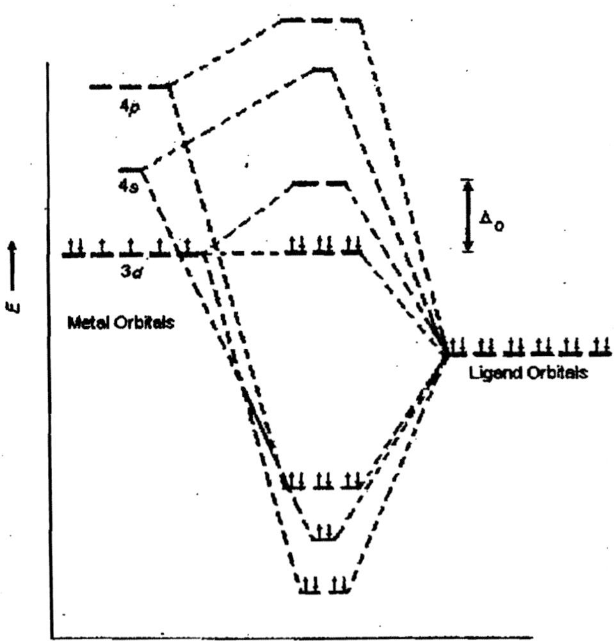

The ligand-field model for an octahedral transition-metal complex such as the $Co(NH_3)_6^{3+}$ ion assumes that the 3*d*, 4*s*, and 4*p* orbitals on the metal overlap with one orbital on each of the six ligands to form a total of 15 molecular orbitals, as shown in the figure on previous page.

Six of these orbitals are *bonding molecular orbitals,* whose energies are much lower than those of the original atomic orbitals. Another six are *antibonding molecular orbitals,* whose energies are higher than those of the original atomic orbitals. Three are best described as *nonbonding molecular orbitals,* because they have essentially the same energy as the 3*d* atomic orbitals on the metal.

Ligand-field theory enables the 3*d*, 4*s*, and 4*p* orbitals on the metal to overlap with orbitals on the ligand to form the octahedral covalent bond skeleton that holds this complex together. At the same time, this model generates a set of five orbitals in the centre of the diagram that are split into $t_{2g}$ and $e_g$ subshells, as predicted by the crystal-field theory. As a result, we don't have to worry about "inner-shell" versus "outer-shell" metal complexes. In effect, we can use the 3*d* orbitals in two different ways. We can use them to form the covalent bond skeleton and then use them again to form the orbitals that hold the electrons that were originally in the 3*d* orbitals or the transition metal.

# 9

# CHARGE TRANSFER SPECTRA

The term, *charge transfer,* implies the movements of an electron from one part of a complex to another. Charge transfer transitions occur as the result of the absorption of a photon of suitable energy to cause such a movement of an electron. The movemnt of charge may be either (i) from an orbital largely localised on the ligands to one largely localised on the metal (LMCT) or (ii) the reverse process (MLCT).

In a complex, there are bonding σ orbitals largely composed of ligand group orbitals with only a minor contribution from any metal orbitals. In addition, there is the possibility of there being π ligand orbitals which may interact with the $t_{2g}$ orbitals of the metal to give bonding and anti-bonding combinations. In such a case, the $t_{2g}$ orbitals become anti-bonding (with respect to the metal-ligand interaction). If the ligands possess anti-bonding π orbitals interaction with the $t_{2g}$ metal orbitals causes the stabilisation of the latter.

## Ligand-metal Charge Transfer Transitions (LMCT)

Fig. 9.1 shows the four types of possible LMCT transitions which may be classified as follows.

(i) $L(\sigma) \rightarrow M(t_{2g})$

(ii) $L(\sigma) \rightarrow M(e_g{*})$

(iii) $L(\pi) \rightarrow M(t_{2g})$

(iv) $L(\pi) \rightarrow M(e_g{*})$

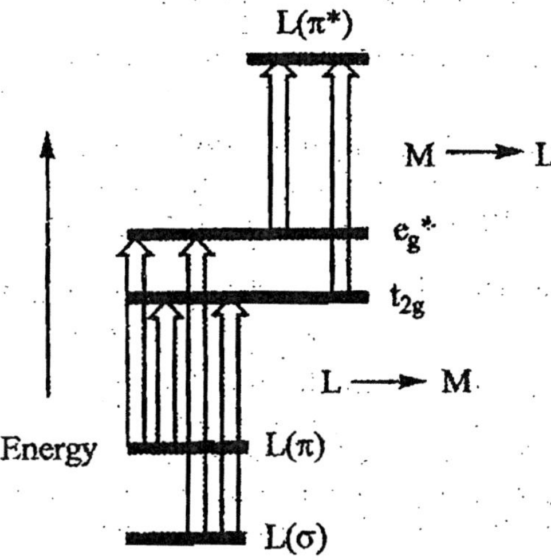


Fig. 9.1: The various charge transfer transitions which can occur in complexes.

Classes (i) and (iii) are impossible if there is a $t_{2g}^6$ configuration and are limited to those comlexes with fewer than six $t_{2g}$ electrons. None of the transitions is possible for $d^{10}$ complexes. The transitions are usually of high intensity since the ligand group orbital combinations contain *u*-type representations.

The highly coloured compunds containing the ions, $VO_4^{3-}$, $CrO_4^{2-}$ and $MnO_4^-$, are examples of $d^0$ metal centres to which electron transfers from the oxide ligands cause their respective characteristic spectra in the visible region.

## Metal-ligand Charge Transfer Transitions (MLCT)

Fig. 9.1 shows the two classes of possible metal-ligand charge transfer transitions:

(i) $M(e_g*) \rightarrow L\ (\pi*)$

(ii) $M(t_{2g})\ (\pi)\ L\ (\pi*)$

which may occur. These transitions are available in those complexes in which there is π back bonding (unsaturated ligands). The existence of class (i) depends upon the anti-bonding $e_g$*

orbitals being occupied in the ground state. As the π group orbitals contain *u*-type representations the MLCT transitions are allowed and are observed to have high intensities.

The detailed interpretations of charge transfer spectra are complicated. The complications arise from two sources. One is that the ligand orbitals (π and/or π*) may form group orbitals so that several states are produced. The other is that some of the charge transfer bands may be obscured by π-π* transitions between various ligand orbitals. Examples of CT spectra follow.

The hexaiodoosmium(IV) ion, $OsI_6^{2-}$, exhibits intense absorptions at 862-538 nm, 373-281 nm and 224 nm, which are thought to be $\pi$-$t_{2g}$, $\pi$-$e_g$* and $\sigma$-$e_g$* LMCT transitions respectively. The tris-1, 10-phenanthrolineiron(II) ion, $[Fe(phen)_3]^{2+}$, ehibits intense absorptions at 520 nm, 320 nm and 290 nm. They are MLCT transitions. Any higher energy MLCT transitions are obscured by the two intra-ligand π-π* transitions of the ligand system which are observed at 229 and 263 nm.

# 10

# MOLECULAR ORBITAL TREATMENT OF COMPLEXES WITH OCTAHEDRAL TREATMENT

## Introduction

In this treatment, emphasis is placed upon the relative energies of the d orbitals since they lose their free-atomic five-fold degeneracy in the presence of an environment of ligands of non-spherical symmetry. This has consequences for the electronic spectra and magnetic properties of the complexes so formed.

## Complexes with Octahedral symmetry

A complex such as $[FeF_6]^{3-}$ possesses true octahedral symmetry ($O_h$) in that the ligands are monatomic. Complexes with molecular ligands, such as $[Co(NH_3)_6]^{3+}$, are not strictly octahedral. In such a case, the random orientations of the hydrogen atoms of the six ammonia ligands as the molecules undergo rotational and vibrational motion prevents the complex from having true octahedral symmetry at any particular time. Such motion by the ligands does not seem to be important. Either the rotational and vibrational motions of the non-ligated atoms produce a satistical balancing effect or the effects upon the d orbitals are produced by the 'local' symmetry of the donor atoms. The replacement of the six monodentate ammonia ligands of the $[Co(NH_3)_6]^{3+}$ complex by three bidentate (because the molecule prossesses two donor nitrogen atoms) diaminoethane ($NH_2CH_2CH_2NH_2$ =en) ligands does not alter the 3d orbital energies significantly even though the $[Co(en)_3]^{3+}$ complex has only $D_3$ symmetry. It would appear that the local symmetry (approximating to $O_h$) of the six ligating nitrogen atoms is predominant in affecting the 3d orbitals of the cobalt(III) ion at the centre of the complex.

## Molecular Orbital Treatment of $ML_6$ ($O_h$) Complexes

The molecular orbital treatment of an $ML_6$ complex follows the usual pattern of classifying the orbitals of the central metal atom, and the ligand group orbitals, with respect to the $O_h$ point group, and allowing those orbitals with the same symmetry to form bonding and anti-bonding combinations.

The orbitals of the central metal atom are, for a member of the first transition series, the 4s, 3d and 4p atomic orbitals. They transform, with respect to the $O_h$ point group, as follows:

| | |
|---|---|
| 4s(M): | $a_{1g}$ |
| $3d_{xy,xzyz}$(M): | $t_{2g}$ |
| $3d_{z2}$, $3d_{x^2-y^2}$(M): | $e_g$ |
| $4p_{xyz}$ (M): | $t_{1u}$ |

The six s orbitals from the six ligands may be placed in diametrically opposed pairs along the Cartesian axes. In Fig. 10.1 the positive y portions of those orbitals are shown.

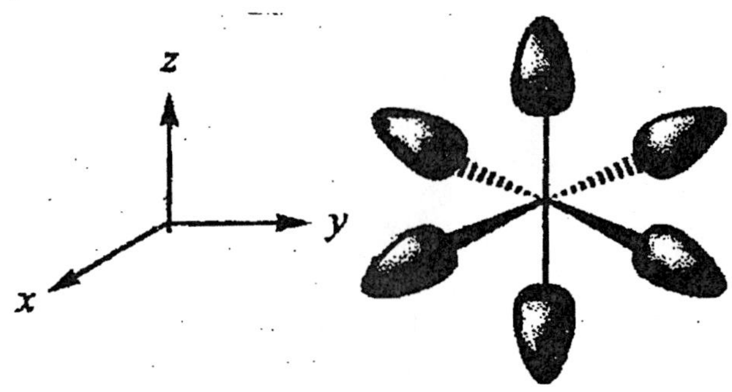


Fig. 10.1: Ligand orbitals in an octahedral complex.

Their character with respect to the symmetry operations of the $O_h$ point group may be written down in the usual fashion in terms of the number of orbitals unaffected by each operation:

| | $E$ | $C_3$ | $C_2$ | $C_4$ | $C_2$ | $i$ | $S_4$ | $S_6$ | $\sigma_h$ | $\sigma_d$ |
|---|---|---|---|---|---|---|---|---|---|---|
| $6 \times \sigma(L)$ | 6 | 0 | 0 | 2 | 2 | 0 | 0 | 0 | 4 | 2 |

Some indication of the disposition of the various elements of symmetry is helpful in understanding the derivation of the above character. The $C_3$ axes are best visualised as passing through the centre of the triangular faces of the octahedron and the central atom of the complex. Rotation around such an axis by 120° moves all six orbitals. The $C_2$ axes are those which bisect any two of the Cartesian axes and lie in one or other of the planes, *xy*,*xz* or *yz*. Rotation around such an axis by 180° affects all six σ orbitals of the ligands. The $C_4$ axes are the three which are coincident with the Cartesian axes and each contain the central metal atom and two diametrically opposed ligand atoms. Rotation around such an axis by 90° leaves the two ligand orbitals, centred on that axis, unchanged. The next $C_2$ axes are those which are coincident with the $C_4$ axes—rotation around them by 180° leaves two ligand orbitals unchanged.

The operation of inversion causes all six ligand orbitals to move. The $S_4$ axes are co-axial with the $C_2$ axes which bisect the pairs of Cartesian axes. The $S_4$ operation moves all six ligand orbitals. The $S_6$ axes are co-axial with the $C_3$ axes. The $S_6$ operation moves all six ligand orbitals.

Reflexion of the six ligand orbitals through any of the three horizontal planes of symmetry (represented by the *xy*, *xz* and *yz* planes) leaves four of the ligand orbitals (the ones in the particular plane chosen) unaffected by the operation. The dihedral planes (there are six) bisect the pairs of horizontal planes (each of which contains a $C_2$ axis) and reflexion in any one of them causes four ligand orbitals to move, leaving two unaffected.

The character of the six σ ligand orbitals is reducible to the sum:

$$6 \times \sigma\,(L) = a_{1g} + e_g + t_{1u}$$

The $a_{1g}$ and $t_{1u}$ combinations have the correct symmetries for interaction with the 4s and 4p orbitals, respectively, of the metal atom. Likewise the $e_g$ orbitals of the ligands and the metal atom may combine to give bonding and anti-bonding orbitals. The remaining $t_{2g}$ orbitals of the metal atom are non-bonding in a s only complex. A s-only m.o. diagram is shown in Fig. 10.2.

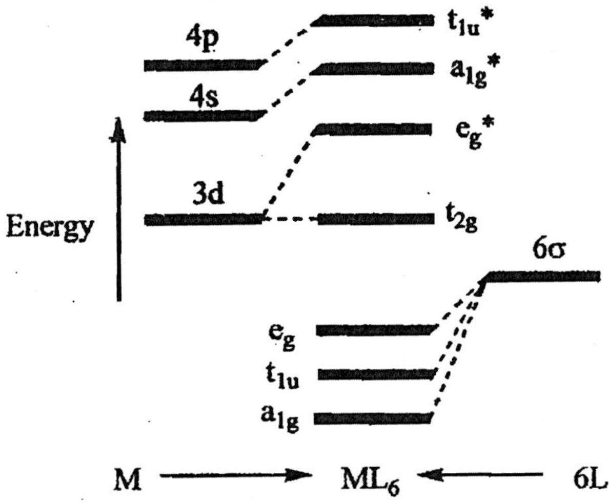


Fig. 10.2: A sigma-orbital only molecular orbital diagram for an octahedral complex

It is conventional in this area of m.o. theory to dispense with the Mulliken numbering of levels and to use asterisks (*) to indicate anti-bonding character.

Such a bonding scheme is very helpful in explaining the spectroscopic and magnetic properties of a wide range of complexes. The main determinant of those properties is the energy difference between the anti-bonding $e_g$* and the non-bonding $t_{2g}$ orbitals. Such a gap in energy allows for *d-d electronic transitions* which happen to lie mainly in the visible region of the electromagnetic spectrum and account largely for the highly colourful chemistry observed for most transition metal complexes.

The energy gap referred to above is the equivalent of the $\Delta_{octahedral}$, or $\Delta_{oct}$ or $\Delta_o$ (or sometimes 10Dq) or crystal field theory (which treats ligands as though they are point charges).

The magnetic properties of any compound depend upon the number of unpaired electrons it possesses. Consider the hexaaquo(III) ion, $[Fe(H_2O)_6]^{3+}$, in which there are five electrons supplied by the $Fe^{III}$ ion and twelve electrons by the six water ligands making a total of seventeen electrons to be placed in the molecular orbitals of Fig. 10.2.

If the *aufbau* principle is obeyed this would lead to the electronic configuration:

$$[Fe(H_2O)_6]^{3+} : a_{1g}{}^2 t_{1u}{}^6 e_g{}^4 t_{2g}{}^5$$

In this configuration, the five electrons of highest energy enter the triply degenerate $t_{2g}$ orbitals with one of the electrons being unpaired. The pairing of electrons in the $t_{2g}$ orbitals would only occur if the energy gap between the anti-bonding $e_g{}^\star$ level and the $t_{2g}$ orbitals were to the sufficient to enforce pairing in the lower level. For the example in question, this does not seem to be the case because the complex has a magnetic moment which indicates that there are *five* unpaired electrons, rather than the single unpaired electron which would result from a $t_{2g}{}^5$ configuration. The manner in which the five electrons may be distributed so that they may occupy orbitals singly is to make use of the anti-bonding $e_g{}^\star$ orbitals to give the configuration: $t_{2g}{}^3$ $(e_g{}^\star)$. In compliance with Hund's rules the five electrons have parallel spins which is consistent with the observed magnetic moment. The energy gap between the $e_g{}^\star$ and $t_{2g}$ orbitals in the complex, $[Fe(H_2O)_6]^{3+}$, must be smaller than the interelectronic repulsion energy which would be experienced in the $t_{2g}{}^5$ configuration plus the loss of exchange energy from 10*K* to 4*K* when pairing occurs. This conclusion arises from the following calculation.

The energy of the $t_{2g}{}^5$ configuration is given by:

$$E(t_{2g}{}^5) = -5E(t_{2g}) + 2P - 4K \qquad (1)$$

where $P$ is the increase in internuclear repulsion energy or pairing energy when two otherwise unpaired electrons pair up in one orbital and $K$ is the unit of exchange energy between two electrons of the same spin. In the $t_{2g}^5$ configuration there are two electrons with one spin and three electrons with the opposite spin. The pair of electrons are stabilised by one unit of exchange energy and the triplet of electrons are stabilised by $3K$ since there are three pair-wise interactions in that case. In general the number of pair-wise interactions between $n$ electrons of the same spin is given by the value of ${}^nC_2 = n!/(2!(n-2)!)$, i.e. the number of combinations of two electrons, the particles being indistinguishable from each other.

The energy of the $t_{2g}^3\ (e_g^\star)^2$ configuration is given by:

$$E(t_{2g}^3(e_g^\star)^2) = -3E\ (t_{2g}) + 2(-E(t_{2g})+\Delta) - 10K = -5E(t_{2g}) + 2\Delta - 10K \quad (2)$$

The difference in energy between the two possible configurations is thus:

$$E(t_{2g}^3(e_g^\star)^2) - E(t_{2g}^5) = -5E(t_{2g}) + 2\Delta - 10K - (-5E(t_{2g}) + 2P - 4K)$$
$$= 2\Delta - 2P - 6K \quad (3)$$

If the value of $\Delta$ is less than $P + 3K$ the $t_{2g}^3(e_g^\star)^2$ configuration will be more stable than the $t_{2g}^3$ one and a high spin state results. On the other hand, if the value of $\Delta$ is larger than $P+3K$ pairing will result to give $t_{2g}^5$ as the more stable configuration, a low spin state. In the latter case the large $\Delta$ value counteracts the loss of energy due to the pairing of four electrons and the loss of $6K$ of exchange energy stabilisation.

The $d^4$ case is another example of the possibility of spin pairing occurring if the value of $\Delta$ is sufficiently large. The energy of the high spin $t_{2g}^3\ (e_g^\star)^1$ configuration is given by:

$$E(t_{2g}^3(e_g^\star)^1) = -3E\ (t_{2g}) + (-E(t_{2g}) + \Delta) - 6K = -4E\ (t_{2g}) + \Delta - 6K \quad (4)$$

That of the low spin $t_{2g}^4$ is given by:

$$E\ (t_{2g}^4) = -4E\ (t_2g) + P - 3K \quad (5)$$

A plot of the two equations as functions of Δ shows that the high spin is lower in energy than the high spin case if $\Delta = 0$, but as Δ increases in value a cross-over occurs making it the less stable configuration.

Both *P* and *K* are difficult to estimate and so the decision as to whether pairing in the $d^{4-7}$ cases occurs is generally made by considering the experimentally derived values of Δ and magnetic moment of the complex under study.

The complexes of iron(III) and cobalt(III) with six ligands which are either fluoride ion, $F^-$, ammonia or cyanide ion, $CN^-$, serve to extend this discussion. A summary of the magnetic properties of the six possible homoleptic (i.e. where are metal ion is complexed by only one particular ligand) $ML_6$ complexes is shown in Table 10.1.

The substitution of $F^-$ ion for $NH_3$ in the $Fe^{III}$ complex has no effect upon the electron arrangement, but the substitution of $CN^-$ causes electron pairing to be preferable to population of the $e_g{}^\star$ level.

**Table 10.1**
**The numbers of unpaired electrons for some metal ion-ligand combinations**

| Ligands | $F^{III}$, $d^5$ | $Co^{III}$, $d^6$ |
|---|---|---|
| $6F^-$ | 5 | 4 |
| $6NH_3$ | 5 | 0 |
| $6CN^-$ | 1 | 0 |

The pattern is somewhat different in the case of the cobalt(III) complexes, where both the ammonia and cyanide complexes have a large enough $e_g{}^\star$-$t_{2g}$ energy gap to enforce electron pairing. It is clear that the energy gap depends upon the nature of the metal ion (it also depends upon the oxidation state of the metal, see later) as well as upon the nature of the ligand. Observations of the visible spectra of complexes allow estimates of the energy gap to be made and the results are shown in Table 10.2.

Table 10.2
$e_g$*-$t_{2g}$ energy differences for some metal ion-ligand combinations/kJ mol-1

| Ligands | $Fe^{III}$, $d^5$ | $Co^{III}$, $d^5$ |
|---|---|---|
| $6F^-$ | 150 | 196 |
| $6NH_3$ | 209 | 272 |
| $6CN^-$ | 285 | 370 |

By comparing the data in Tables 10.1 and 10.2 it is clear that electron pairing takes place (in these systems) when the $e_g$*-$t_{2g}$ gap is greater than ~ 270 kJ $mol^{-1}$.

In general ligands have the same relative effect upon the $e_g$*$t_{2g}$ splitting irrespective of the metal ion. Some common ligands in the order of their increasing splitting effect are: $I^-$ <$Br^-$ < $Cl^-$ ~$SCN^-$ (ligand atom, S) < $F^-$ < $OH^-$ < $C_2O_4^{2-}$ ~ $H_2O$ <edta<$NCS^-$ (ligand atom, N) ~ $H^-$ < $NH_3$ ~ py < en < $NO_2^-$ (ligand atom, N) < bipy < phen < CO ~ $C_2H_4$ ~ $CN^-$ (phen is the abbreviation for 1, 10-phenanthroline). There are negative ligands at either end of this series and neutral ligands in between. The more basic (in terms of the Lewis base electron pair donation sense of the term) ligands are centrally placed in the series. The series itself is called the *spectrochemical series*. This is because the values upon which it is based are derived from measurements of absorption spectra, from which the $e_g$*-$t_{2g}$ energy gaps may be determined.

The variations in the $e_g$*-$t_{2g}$ energy gap may be understood in terms of the relative basicities (in terms of electron pair donation tendency) of the ligands and the type of π-type bonding which is involved. The more basic the ligand the stronger will be the bonding and the larger the $e_g$*-$t_{2g}$ gap should be. The effects of π–bonding explain why the cyanide ion, and the neutral CO molecule, with low basicity are at the top end of the spectrochemical series.

There are two cases of π-bonding to be considered. These are:

(i) $\pi$ donation of electrons from the ligand to the metal atom, and

(ii) $\pi$ donation of electrons from the metal atom to the ligand.

## Ligand-to-metal Atom p Donation of Electrons

Fig. 10.3 shows the possible overlap between a metal atom $d_{xy}$ orbital (one of the $t_{2g}$ set) and a ligand $p_x$ orbital.

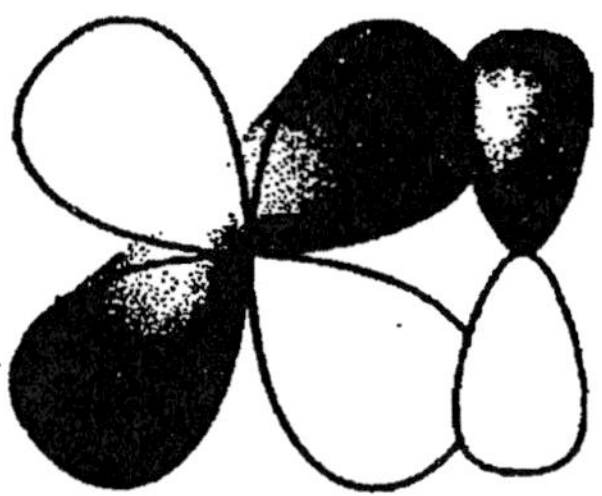

**Fig. 10.3:** The pi-overlap of a metal $d_{xz}$ orbital with a ligand $p_z$ orbital in the *xz* plane.

It is clear from the signs of $\psi$ (positive shaded, negative white) that such an overlap would lead to m.o. formation. Ligand p orbitals are usually doubly occupied so that for any $\pi$-interaction to be energetically advantageous it is necessary for the $t_{2g}$ orbitals of the metal ion to be either vacant or only singly occupied. Such interaction can only be advantageous for the $t_{2g}^{0-3}$ configurations of metals-where any electrons in excess of three must occupy the $e_g$★ orbitals (i.e. high spin $d^{4-5}$ configurations).

The energies of the ligand orbitals which engage in ligand-metal $\pi$-bonding are normally lower than those of the $t_{2g}$ orbitals of the metal. This means that when $\pi$ -interaction occurs the lower (bonding) orbitals have a majority contribution from the ligand orbitals. The higher (anti-bonding) combinations have energies greater than those of the original $t_{2g}$ orbitals (which should be labelled strictly as $t_{2g}$★) and, in consequence, the $e_g$★-$t_{2g}$★ energy gap is reduced. The effect is shown on the left-hand side of Fig. 10.4.

## Metal Atom-Ligand $\pi$ Donation of Electrons

The cyanide ion and the carbon monoxide molecule are isoelectronic and possess occupied $\pi_u$ bonding orbitals and vacant anti-bonding $\pi_g$* orbitals. The latter orbitals may interact with the metal $t_{2g}$ orbitals to give metal-ligand bonding and anti-bonding $\pi$ m.o.'s.

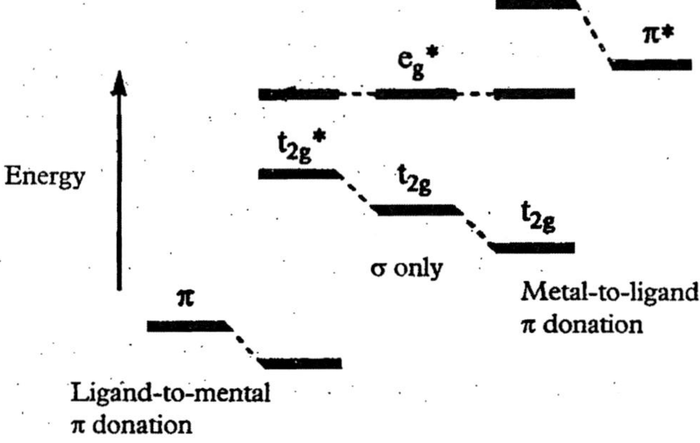


**Fig. 10.4:** A molecular orbital diagram showing the effects of $\pi$ interaction on the energy of the $t_{2g}$ orbitals of an octahedral complex.

The anti-bonding ligand $\pi_g$* orbitals are normally of higher energies than the metal $t_{2g}$ orbitals, so it is the latter which contribute more to the metal-ligand $\pi$ bonding orbitals. The ligand $\pi_g$* orbitals have a major contribution to the metal-ligand anti-bonding m.o.'s. This has the effect of increasing the $e_g$*-$t_{2g}$* energy gap as is shown on the right-hand side of Fig. 10.4.

This ligand-to-metal donation of electrons is sometimes known as $\pi$ **back donation,** as if to offset the normal or forward ligand-metal donation. Another description of the same phenomenon is $\pi$-acid behaviour of the ligand, one definition of an acid being that it is a compound which has electron-pair accepting properties. The back donation effect explains, in electronic terms, the production of relatively strong bonds by such ligands as $CN^-$ and CO. Their normal tendency to be weakly basic is overcome because any loss of electron pairs by ligand-metal donation is balanced, to some extent, by the metal-ligand back donation. One effect feeds the other and is known as *synergism.* The *synergic effect* of one type of bonding reinforcing the other contributes to very strong bonding and a very large $\Delta_0$ value.

Complexes with back bonding are produced when the metal $t_{2g}$ orbitals are filled so that the electrons therein are stabilised by the formation of the π-orbitals providing that suitable receptor orbitals are available on the ligands.

The ethene molecule, $C_2H_4$, bonds strongly to some metal ions in a side-ways-on mode. Because of the terminal C-H bonds it does not have any σ orbitals which could be used in ligand-metal donation. It does, however, possess filled $\pi_u$ C-C bonding orbitals, the electrons of which may be used to form a ligand-metal sigma bond.

## The John-Teller Effect

The Jahn-Teller effect applies to complexes with an odd number of electrons in the $e_g$* or $t_{2g}$ orbitals. It is more important in the $e_g$* cases (because the orbitals have a greater interaction with the ligands) and, as such, it concerns the electronic configurations: high spin $d^4$, low spin $d^7$, and $d^9$, with $(e_g{*})^1$, $(e_g{*})^1$ and $(e_g{*})^3$ configurations respectively. It may be stated in the form: 'If, in a non-linear molecular, a degenerate set of orbitals is unevenly occupied, and a distortion is possible which removes their degeneracy, then such a distortion will occur and lead to a stabilisation of the system.'

In the case of regularly octahedral complexes which possess the doubly degenerate $e_g$* anti-bonding level the distortion which usually occurs is where two of the bonds (along the z direction) become elongated, and the four bonds in the square plane (*xy*) are shortened. Such a distortion causes the symmetry to change from $O_h$ to $D_{4h}$ and the $e_g$* orbitals lose their two-fold degeneracy. The orbital with the $d_{z^2}$ contribution becomes stabilised (the ligands are further away from the metal ion along the z axis) and

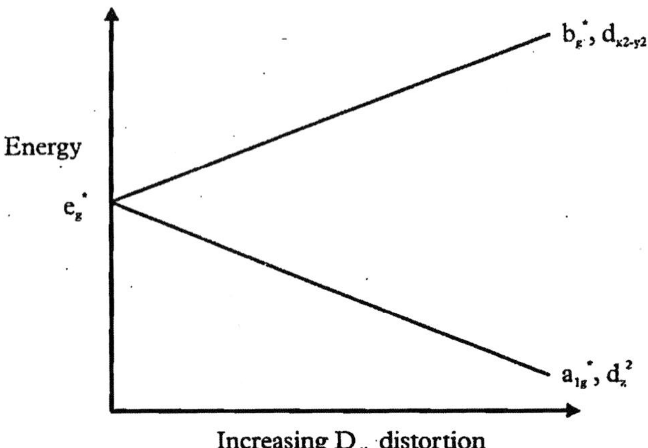


Fig. 10.5: The Jahn-Teller effect on the energies of the $e_g$* orbitals as $D_{4h}$ distortion increases (to give four shortened bonds and two longer ones).

is labelled $a_{1g}$*. The orbital with the $d_{x^2-y^2}$ is destabilised (the ligands are nearer the metal in the *xy* plane) and becomes the $b_{1g}$* orbital. Fig. 10.5 demonstrates these effects.

The distortion to give the more stable $a_{1g}$* orbital leads to the 'distorted' complex being more stable than the regular octahedral form when it is possible for there to be more electrons in it than occupy the destabilised $b_{1g}$* orbital.

The reverse effect produced by a distortion of the two short bond, four long bond configuration of a complex does occur but only in the solid state where crystal packing effects are an added consideration.

The case of the even filling of the $e_g$* orbitals of an $O_h$ complex may lead to stabilisation by distortion to $D_{4h}$ symmetry only if the distortion is sufficient to force electron pairing in the lower $a_{1g}$ orbital. If the difference in energy between the $b_{1g}$* and $a_{1g}$* orbitals is sufficiently high then an $(e_g*)^2$ $(O_h)$ configuration would be more stable as $(a_{1g}*)$ $(D_{4h})$ with consequent changes in geometry and in magnetic properties. Such an effect is only observed in square planar complexes which may be thought of as distorted octahedral complexes with two infinitely long bonds along the z axis.

## Molecular Orbital Treatment of Square Planar, $D_{4h}$, Complexes

The complex is set up with its $C_4$ axis coincident with the z axis. Inspection of the $D_{4h}$ character table allows the classification of the orbitals of the central metal ion as follows:

| | |
|---|---|
| 4s(M): | $a_{1g}$ |
| $3d_{xy}$(M): | $b_{2g}$ |
| $3d_{z^2}$(M): | $a_{1g}$ |
| $3d_{x^2-y^2}$(M): | $b_{1g}$ |
| $3d_{xzyz}$(M): | $e_g$ |
| $4p_z$(M): | $a_{2u}$ |
| $4p_{xy}$(M): | $e_u$ |

so that mixing of the 4s and $3d_z2$ orbitals is possible. The reduction of the symmetry from $O_h$ to $D_{4h}$ causes there to be more irreducible representations to deal with, and with a consequent lowering of degeneracy, which leads to a more complicated m.o. diagram.

The four σ ligand orbitals lie along the metal-ligand directions (coincident with the *x* and *y* axes) and are classified as:

$$4 \times L(\sigma) = a_{1g} + b_{1g} + e_u$$

The four ligand $p_z$ (or p orbitals with a z component) are classified as:

$$4 \times L(\pi,z) = a_{2u} + b_{2u} + e_g$$

The other four p or π ligand orbitals (those in the *xy* plane at right angles to the metal-ligand directions) have a character which reduces to the sum:

$$4 \times L(\pi, xy) = a_{2g} + b_{2g} + e_u$$

The m.o. diagram, for the *sigma* orbitals only, is shown in Fig. 10.6. As in the case of octahedral complexes there is the possibility of π bonding which would possibly alter the order of the energy levels.

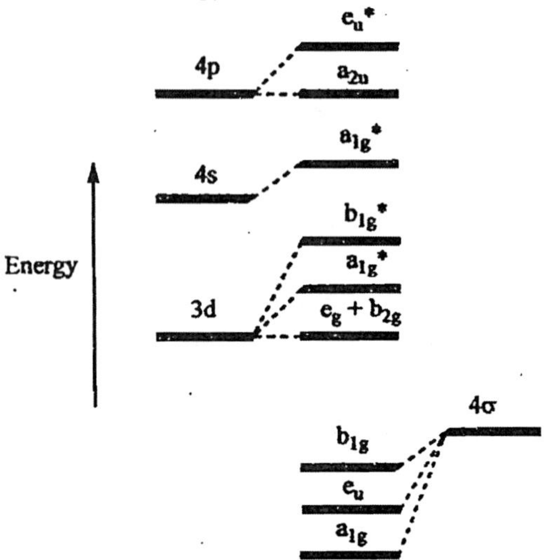


Fig. 10.6: A molecular orbital diagram for a square planar complex (sigma orbitals only).

The bonding of alkenes (the simplest being ethene, $C_2H_4$) to metals is particularly important in square planar complexes. One notable example is that of the trichloro ($\eta^2$-ethene) platinate(II) ion, $[(C_2H_4)PtCl_3]$. The ethene molecule is bonded so that its carbon-carbon axis is perpendicular to the plane containing the platinum(II) and chloride ions. The geometry is shown in Fig. 10.7. The two carbon atoms of the ethene molecule are bonded to, or are within bonding distance of, the platinum centre. It is for this reason that the nomenclature of the complex makes use of the Greek letter eta, η, (from ηαπτειν = haptein, to fasten) with a superscript (2 in this case) to indicate the number of donor atoms bonded to the central metal ion.

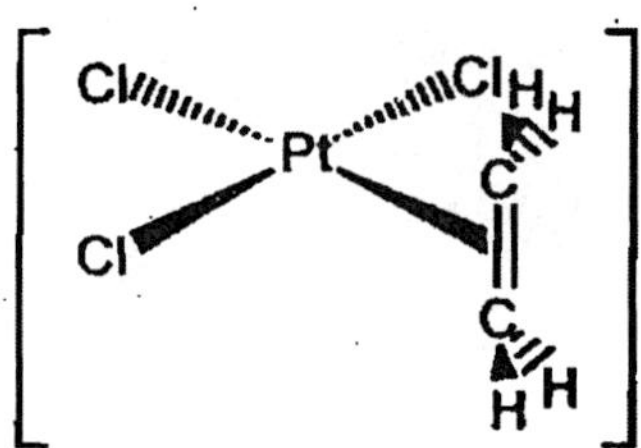


Fig. 10.7: The structure of the trichloro-$\eta^2$-(ethene) platinum(II) ion.

The ethene molecule has a filled π bonding orbital which is in the plane which is perpendicular to the molecular plane and which contains the two carbon atoms. The vacant anti-bonding π* orbital is in the same plane and both are shown in Fig. 10.8. It is possible for electrons to be donated to a σ platinum orbital ($d_{x^2-y^2}$ is used in Fig. 10.8) forming an ethene-platinum bond. The ethene-to-plantinum electron-pair donation reduces the effectiveness of the π-bonding between the carbon atoms of the ethene ligand. The $5d_{xz}$ orbital of the platinum has the correct symmetry to form bonding and anti-bonding (Pt-ethene) combinations with the anti-bonding π* orbital of the ethene molecule to promote π back bonding (donation from platinum to ethene) and produce the synergism required to ensure efficient ethene to platinum donation in the σ bonding.

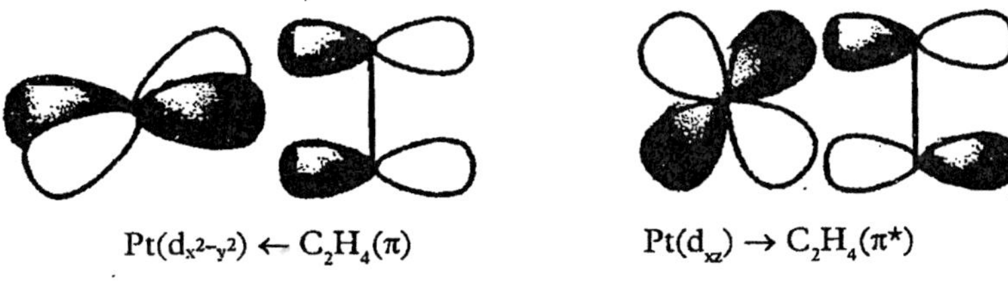


Fig. 10.8: Forward (ethene to Pt) donation and back (Pt to ethene) donation in the bonding between platinum and ethene.

The promotion of an electron from π - π* in a free ethene molecule produces a change of symmetry from $D_{2h}$ to $D_{2d}$ (as would be produced if one $CH_2$ group underwent a 90° rotation with respect to the other). The distortion of the ethene molecule when it acts as a ligand is not consistent with such an electronic transition, the four hydrogen atoms being co-planar due to internuclear repulsion.

Alkenes (and alkynes) do not form complexes with typical acceptor metals (those with vacant π orbitals) but do form many complexes with metals possessing a full $d^{10}$ complement of electrons. In such cases, the ligand to metal donation can only be to the s and p orbitals of the metal. Back donation of a π-type is responsible for the formation of the strong linkages which are observed.

## Molecular Orbital Treatment of Tetrahedral, $T_d$, Complexes

In a tetrahedral environment the orbitals of a central metal atom transform as:

| | |
|---|---|
| 4s(M): | $a_1$ |
| $3d_{xy,xz,yz}$(M): | $t_2$ |
| $3d_{z^2,x^2-y^2}$(M): | e |
| $4p_{xy,z}$ (M): | $t_2$ |

If the four σ ligand orbitals are arranged along the formal metal-ligand directions their character reduces to the sum:

$$4 \times L(\sigma) = a_1 + t_2$$

The other eight ligand (p) orbitals transform as the sum:

$$8 \times L(\pi) = e + t_1 + t_2$$

The m.o. diagram may then be constructed as in Fig. 10.9. There is a low energy $a_1$ m.o. and a higher energy $t_2$ set which is a mixture of σ and π contributions from the ligand orbitals. The ligand $t_1$ set is non-bonding since there are no metal orbitals of that symmetry. Because of the general disposition of the orbitals of the metal and ligands none of the bonding interactions are as efficient as those observed in octahedral and square planar complexes.

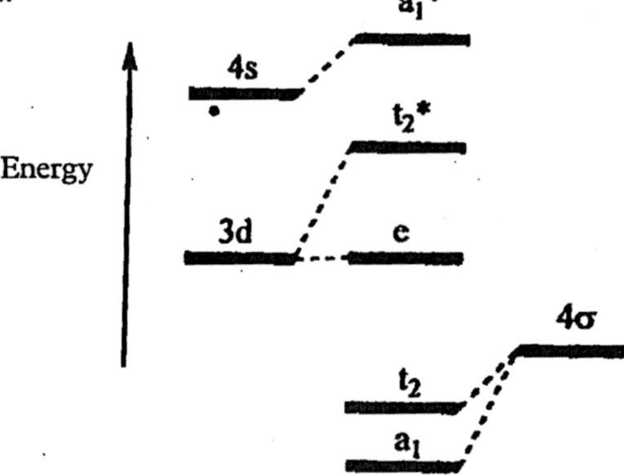


Fig. 10.9: A molecular orbital diagram for a tetrahedral complex.

# 11

# ELECTRONIC ABSORPTION SPECTROSCOPY OF METAL COMPLEXES

Electronic Structure of d-Metal Complexes. One of the most fascination aspects of transition metal complexes is the remarkable specturm of colours which they exhibit. The colours are a result of several features of the complexes which are explicable in reasonably simple terms.

Consider a typical first-transition series metal, e.g., chromium. Free, gaseous charomium atoms have the electronic configuration $1s^2 2s^2 2p^6 3s^2 3p^6 4s^1 3d^5$, or $[Ar]4s^1 3d^5$. Removal of 3 electrons from this atom (remember that 4s electrons come off first, followed by 3d) gives the $Cr^{III}$ ion with configuration $[Ar]3d^3$. Recall that there are five 3d orbitals, each of which can accommodate a maximum of two electrons (one with "up" spin, one with "down" spin). Since for $Cr^{III}$ there are only three electrons to occupy a total of 10 spots, we say that $Cr^{III}$ has "partially filled" d orbitals (the same can be said of a Cr atom). This characteristic is the hallmark of transition metals and their ions and is the primary reason for the colours exhibited by their complexes.

Many transition metal complexes are octahedral, meaning that the metal ion is surrounded by 6 ligands at the vertices of a regular octahedron. We are going to consider what happens to a transition metal ion in this type of environment. For the sake of simplicity, we will consider the ligands to be capable of sigma bonding only--that is, they each have one orbital which contains a pair of electrons and which can overlap along the internuclear axis with a suitable metal orbital. The resulting complex can be pictured as in Figure 11.1, where we have introduced a right-handed Cartesian coordinate system in such a way that the ligands lie along the axes, and we have shown the ligand donor orbitals (e.g., if the ligands were $NH_3$ molecules, these orbitals would by $sp^3$ hybrids) pointing in toward the metal, as they must if effective overlap between ligand and metal orbitals is to occur.

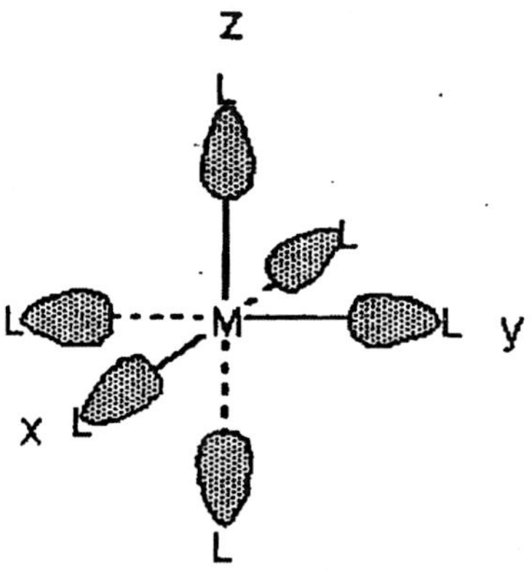


**Figure 11.1**

How will metal and ligand orbitals interact to form molecular orbitals (MOs) for the complex and which metal orbitals will be involved in these MOs?

To answer this question, we must decide which of the metal ion valence orbitals have appropriate shapes and orientations for overlap with the ligand donor orbitals. Consider first the 4s orbital of the metal. Can it overlap in sigma fashion with any of the ligand orbitals? Since the 4s orbital has equal probability density along each of the 6 Cartesian directions, we conclude that, yes, it can overlap with all of the ligand orbitals in $\sigma$ fashion, as shown in Figure 11.2.

Similarly, we conclude that the 4px orbital can overlap in $\sigma$ fashion with both ligand orbitals which lie along the x axis (but not with ligand orbitals along y or z, since the 4px orbital has no probability density along either of these axes); the 4py orbital can

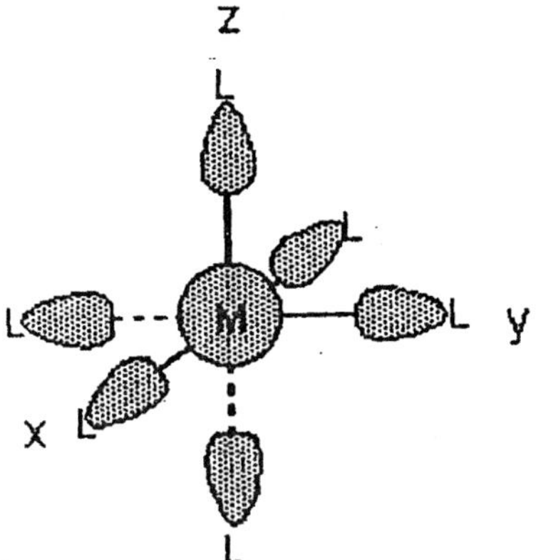


Figure 11.2

overlap with both ligand orbitals along the y axis; and the 4pz orbital can overlap with both ligand orbitals along the z axis. The picture drawn in Figure 11.3 represents any one of the three axes:

Figure 11.3

There is one more point to be made here. You will recall that one label of a p orbital has positive sign, while the other lobe has negative sign. Two orbitals which are to overlap effectively must have the same sign, so the ligand orbital which is to overlap with the negative lobe of the p orbital must be negative, as shown above. This will not concern us any more at this point.

So far we have decided that the 4s and the three 4p orbitals of the metal are all suitable for $\sigma$ bonding with the ligands. However, there are six ligands and thus far we have only 4 metal orbitals to use in bonding them. We need a total of 6 metal orbitals to $\sigma$ bond to 6 ligands. We must therefore decide whether any of the 3d orbitals are located suitably for bonding. Let's consider first the $3d_{z^2}$ orbital, which has positive lobes along the +z and -z directions, and a negative doughnut of probability density in the x-y plane, as shown in Figure 11.4.

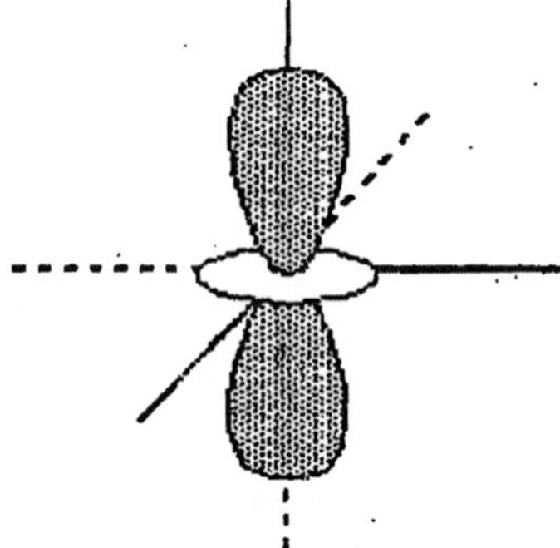

Figure 11.4

The ligand orbitals lying along the z axis can obviously overlap in å fashion with the two positive lobes; and the ligand orbitals approaching along the x and y axes can overlap in å style with the negative doughnut (if we change their signs). We therefore conclude that the $3d_{z^2}$ orbital can engage in σ bonding. Similar conclusions are reached for the $3d_{x^2-y^2}$ orbital, which has positive lobes along +x and -x and negative lobes along +y and -y.

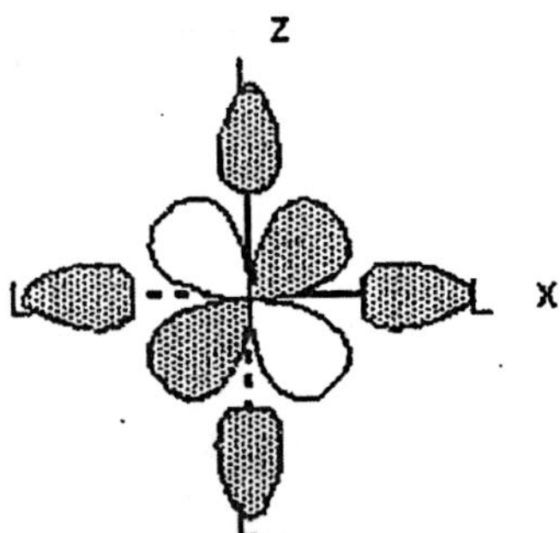


Figure 11.5

We one have found 6 metal orbitals which are capable of σ bonding to the 6 ligands. But we still have not considered any of the three remaining d orbitals—dxy, dyz, dxz. We will consider one of them. Arguments for the other two are identical. Let's consider dxz, which lies in the x-z plane as shown in Figure 11.6.

Consider the ligand σ orbital which is approaching along the +x axis. Can it overlap in σ fashion with dxz? The answer is no. The ligand orbital will overlap with the upper right positive lobe of dxz, but this overlap will be exactly cancelled by an equal and opposite overlap with the lower right negative lobe of dxz. The net overlap is precisely zero. This is equivalent to saying that the dxz orbital has a node along the x axis.

++ overlap combined
With +- overlap adds
up to zero overlap

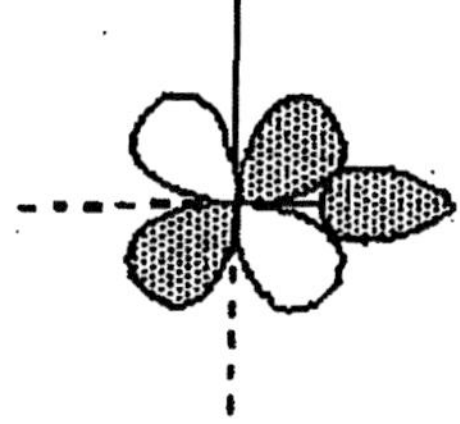

Figure 11.6

Similar arguments show that none of the four ligands in the xz plane have net overlap with dxz, dyz and dxy fail to overlap with ligand σ orbitals for exactly the same reasons. These three orbitals are thus non-bonding in a sigma sense. We conclude that of the originally degenerate (same energy) five 3d orbitals, two are suitable for sigma bonding with ligands and three are not. The d orbitals can therefore be categorised into two groups with respect to their behaviour toward σ -bonding ligands. Are these two groups still of the same energy?

It must be assumed that if two orbitals, even if intrinsically similar, are differently oriented toward their surroundings, there will be some difference in the energy of an electron depending upon which of them it occupies. Let us see precisely why this difference arises. When each of two atoms has an orbital directed toward the other one (say σ 1 and σ 2 of Figure 11.7), and these atoms approach closely enough for these orbitals to overlap, the orbitals become "mixed" to form new orbitals, one (the "bonding molecular orbital" or "bonding MO") having relatively high probability density between the two nuclei, and the other (the "antibonding mlecular orbital" or "antibonding MO") having relatively low probability density between nuclei. When electrons occupy the bonding orbital, the atoms become bound together, while when electrons occupy the antibonding orbital, a repulsive or antibonding force is set up. Two general statements can be made regarding the two molecular orbitals: 1. The bonding MO always has an energy lower than that of either atomic (or hybrid) orbital from which it is formed, and the antibonding MO always has an energy higher than that of either constituent atomic orbital; 2. If the two atomic orbitals with which we begin have rather different energies, the resulting bonding MO will have predominantly the characteristics of the lower energy atomic orbital, while the resulting antibonding MO will have predominantly the characteristics of the higher energy atomic orbital. These two satements are illustrated on an energy leval diagram below.

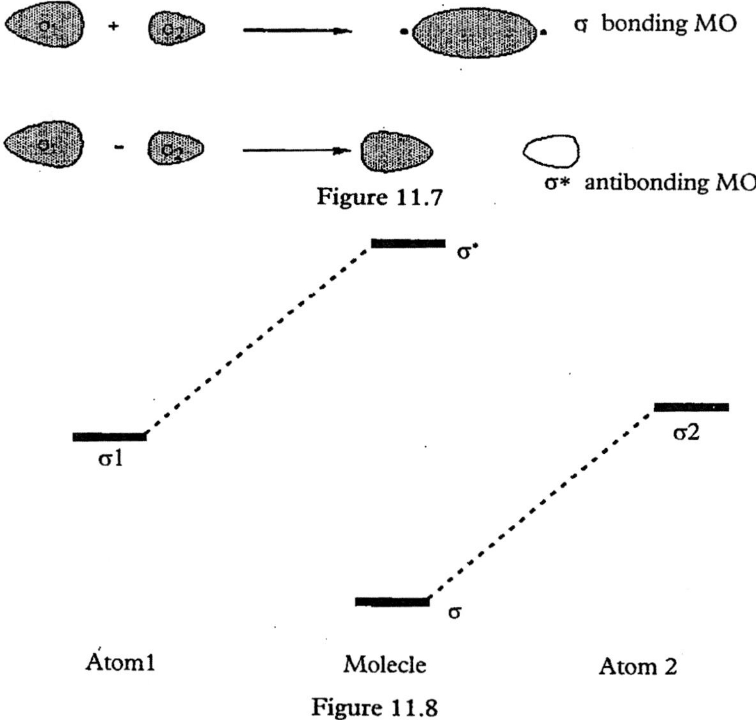


Figure 11.7

Figure 11.8

Finally, we should state that if two atomic or hybrid orbitals are of such a nature that they have no overlap (such as dxz and the ligand σ orbital in Figure 11.6), there is no mixing and no formation of bonding and antibonding orbitals. The two orbitals are said to be non-bonding with respect to each other.

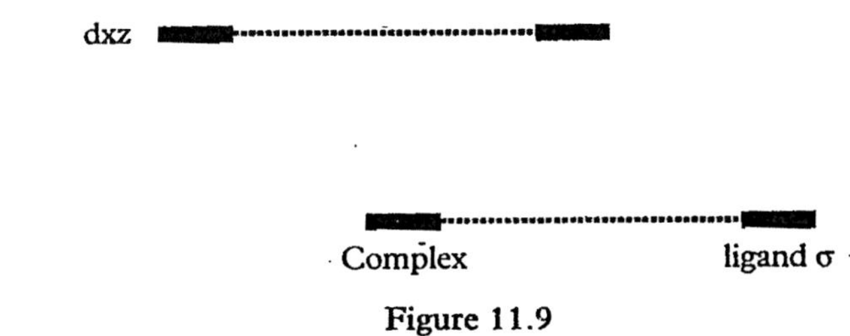


Figure 11.9

All of the above considerations apply not only to diatomic molecules, but also to the case of a metalion interacting in å fashion with six ligands at the apices of an octahedron. Each metal-ligand interaction will give rise to one σ bonding and one σ antibonding MO. Considring only the interaction between the metal d orbitals and the ligand orbitals, the following energy level diagram results:

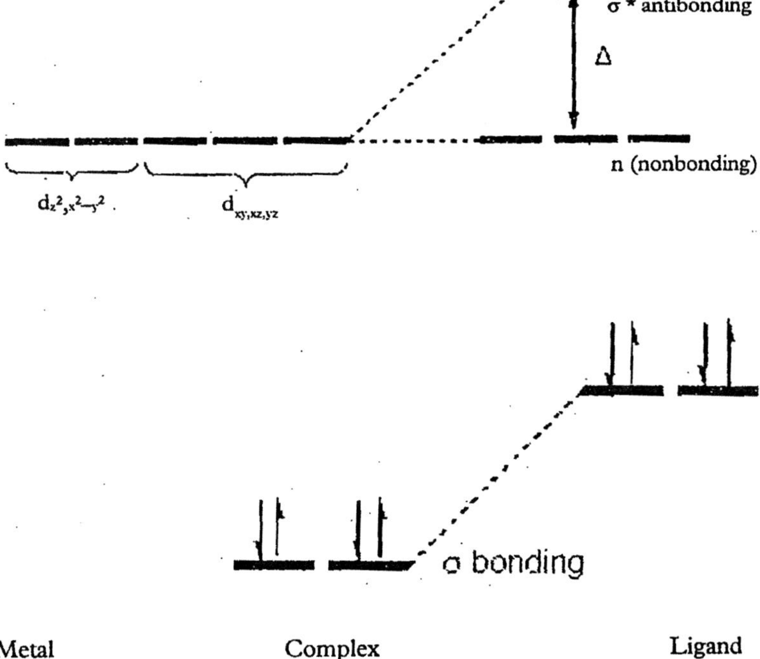


Metal Complex Ligand

Figure 11.10

The $d_{z^2}$ and $d_{x^2-y^2}$ orbitals, which we decided are capable of sigma bonding with the ligands, do so, thus generating two bonding and two antibonding MOs. However, since the metal d orbitals are higher in energy than the ligand sigma orbitals, the antibonding MOs, $\sigma^*$, will have predominantly the character of the metal $d_{z^2}$ and $d_{x^2-y^2}$ orbitals, according to general statement 2 above. The $d_{xy,xy,yz}$ metal orbitals, labelled n, which are impervious to $\sigma$ bonding and are therefore non-bonding, are largely unaffected by bond formation and retain their original energies. So instead of maintaining their original five-fold degeneracy in the complex, the d orbitals are split up into a doubly degenerate set, $\sigma^*$, of higher energy and a triply degenerate set, n, of lower energy. This splitting is labelled and is called the ligand field splitting (LFS) since it arises from the "field" generated by the ligands. Now, each ligand $\sigma$ orbital is originally occupied by a pair of electorns. When the complex is formed, these electron pairs will occupy the molecular orbitals of lowest posssible energy—that is, the $\sigma$ bonding MOs. Occupation of the ligand $\sigma$ orbitals and the $\sigma$ bonding MOs has been indicated in Figure 11.10, where represents an electron pair, one electron with up spin and one with down spin. But how about the d electrons originally possessed by the metal ion—which orbitals will they occupy in the complex? Since the degeneracy of the set of d orbitals has been split, electrons no longer will occupy all members of the set with equal probability. Instead, they tend to occupy the more stable ones preferentially, subject to restrictions arising from the Pauli Exclusion Principle and from interelectronic repulsion. (This is taken up more fully in the chapter dealing with magnetism). The electrons will therefore tend to occupy the triply degenerate non-bonding set first.

Let's return to our original example, Cr $^{III}$. In the complex $Cr(NH_3)_6^{+3}$, the chromium d orbitals will be split as above. The three d electrons originally present on chromium will distribute themselves in the available orbitals of lowest energy, as follows:

If we shine light of suitable energy on a molecule, we can cause an electron to move from its present orbital to an orbital of higher energy. The molecule acquires the energy required to do

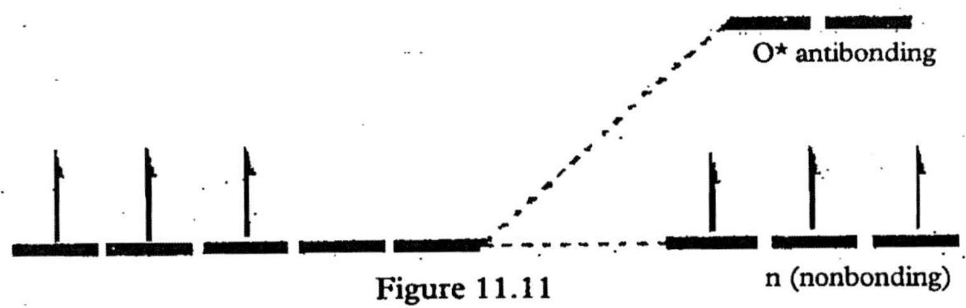


Figure 11.11

this by absorbing a photon of the light, so that not all of the photons which impinge on, say, a solution of the molecule, will emerge from it. If the photons absorbed have frequencies in the visible region of the electromagnetic spectrum (remember, E=hv=hc/λ), the molecule will be coloured. Moreover, the colour that we see will be due to the photons that are not absorbed by the sample--they pass through it and arrive at our eyes. This colour will be the complement of the colour which is absorbed by the molecule. If a compound absorbs light of wavelength 550nm (what is the correspinding frequency? enrgy?), which is green, it will appear to be reddish-blue, or purple. If a compound absorbs light of wavelength 600 nm (yellow), it will appear to us to be blue. The following colour wheel should help you to see this clearly.

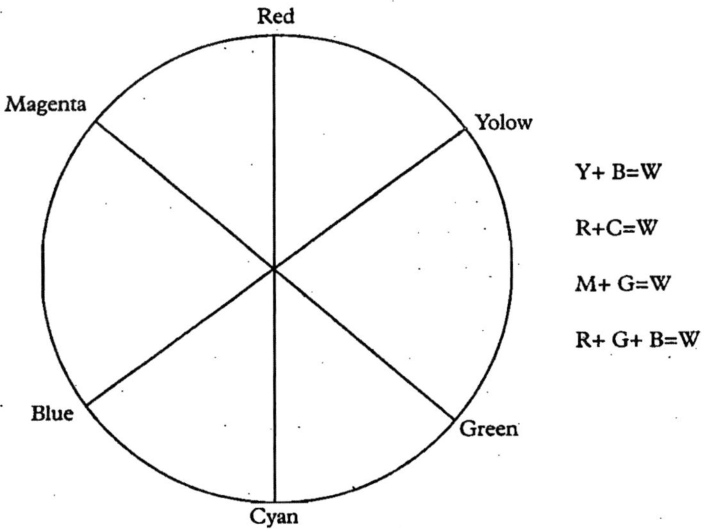


Figure 11.12

Notice that the complement of any colour is directly opposite it on the wheel, and that any colour can be obtained by mixing the two colours on either side of it. Thus a compound which absorbs red + green (=yellow) will appear blue to the eye. (A compound may absorb two colours when it can undergo two different electronic transitions in the visible region). As it happens, the splitting of the d orbitals (the Ligand Field Splitting, $\Delta_o$) in many transition metal complexes is such that visible light is required to cause the transition of an electron from the triply degenerate lower set to the doubly degenerate upper set, $\sigma^*$. (Such a transition is often called a "d-d" transition, since it involves promotion of an electron from one d orbital to another). Whenever this is the case, as we have seen, the complex is coloured. The

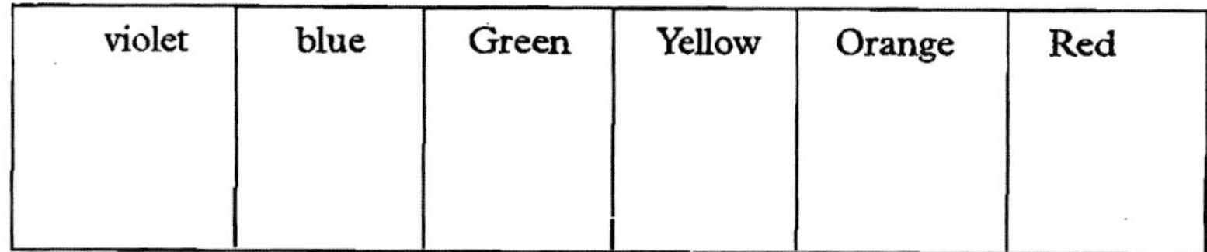


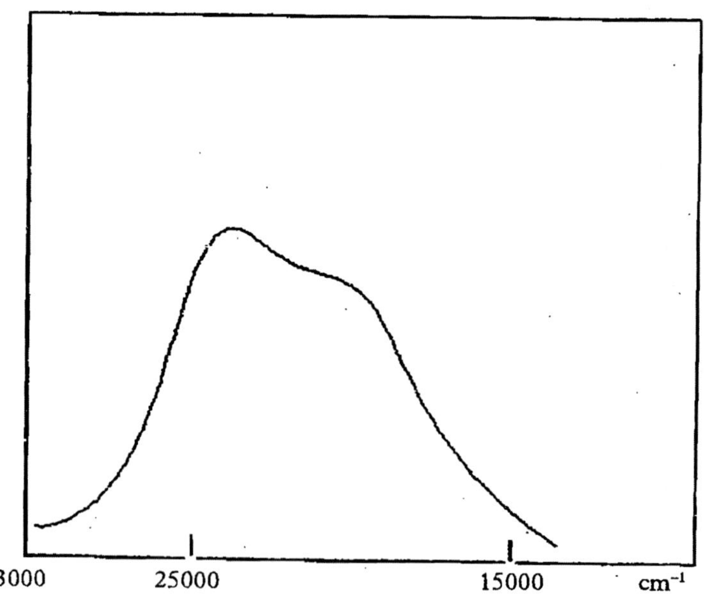


Figure 11.13

following figure illustrates the relationship between colour and the wavelength range of visible light. Included is a spectrum of the Ti $(H_2O)_6^{+3}$ ion, which is purple. As can be seen from the figure 11.13, this ion has an absorption band centered at about 550 nm. It therefore absorbs green, transmits blue and red, and looks purple (blue+red).

This is the explanation for the origin of colour in transition metal complexes--split d orbital which are partially filled. The importance of the latter criterion is nicely illustrated by complexes of $Zn^{II}$, which has the electronic configuration [Ar] $3d^{10}$. d orbital splitting occurs in $Zn^{II}$ just as it does in the $Cr^{III}$ example; however since all d orbital spots are already occupied, no transitions within the d orbitals are possible--hence no colour is absorbed, and the complexes are white.

**Spectrometer Cells.** Cells are containers that are constructed to contain a precise pathlength of solution between two highly polished optical surfaces. Common cell path length for electronic absorption spectroscopy are 10mm (1cm), 50 mm (5 cm), and 100 mm (10 cm). Most commonly used are the 1 cm cells. Cells are supplied by the manufacturer as a matched set, with a set consisting usually of either 2 or 4 cells. The cells of a set must always be used together and never mixed and matched indiscriminately with other sets of cells. One cell of a set is intended to contain sample + solvent, the other to contain just solvent. It does not matter which cell is used for which.

1. Handling
   1. Cells are to be handled by the unpolished faces only. Do not touch the polished faces.
   2. Cells are expensive -->$100 per matched set. When handling them, always do so over a table or bench covered with a towel or cloth, so that if the cell falls from your hand it will not fall far and the blow will be cushioned.
   3. Try to avoid carrying cells directly in your hands. Carry them in their box(es) if at all possible.

2. Cleaning cells
    1. To clean cell faces, wipe them with lens tissue or with a Kimwipe. *Never use a Paper Towel.*
    2. If a solvent is necessary, use a Kimwipe wetted with $H_2O$, acetone or ethanol. Always wipe softly and carefully.
    3. Please do not return a cell to its box until it is completely dry of solvent.
3. Filling Cells
    1. Place the cell carefully on a towel on the bench top.
    2. Hold the cell with the left hand, fill with a Pasteur pipet to within 5 mm of the top. Insert the Pasteur pipet tip no farther than just below the top of the cell. This will prevent scratching of the polished faces with the pipet.
    3. Stopper the cell, dry the outside of any spillage. You are now ready to measure the spectrum.
4. Emptying Cells
    1. Pour the contents of the cell either into a beaker or into the original container. From there it can be either discarded in a waste bottle, or saved.
    2. If it is absolutely necessary to remove the contents of the cell using a Pasteur pipet, do so by inserting the pipet so as not to touch the optical faces.
5. Cleaning cells between runs.
    1. Empty the cell of solution
    2. Rinse the cell a couple of times with the solvent being used. Discard the rinsings.
    3. Rinse the cell with acetone several times.
    4. Aspirate the cell dry.
        * If working in the UV, it is essential to remove all acetone by aspiration, since acetone absorbs in the UV.
        * Never dry a cell by blowing air from the air lines into it, by blowing into it with your mouth, or by waving it around in the air.

Proper choice of cell for the range of interest. There are several types of material used to make cells. These materials differ in the vavelengths of light to which they are transparent. It is important to choose cells of appropriate material for your range. The following list will serve as a guide in choosing the proper cell material.

Optical Glass 320-2600 nm

UV Quartz Glass>220

IR Quartz Glass 270-2730

ES Quartz Glass 200-2000

Quarasil 200-2600

Sample Preparation for EAS. There are two cases to consider

1. Extinction coefficients (e) are known.
    1. Calculate the amount of sample required to prepare a convenient volume of solution (usually 5, 10, or 25 mL) based on ε values of the absorption bands of the sample. Use Beers Law

       $A = \varepsilon cl$

       Substitute the approprite path length and assume that you want an absorbance of 1.
    2. Weigh the required amount of sample into a volumetric flask of appropriate size. The volume of solution to prepare is largely up to you. However, it is generally desirably to prepare the minimum amount of solution required for the job and consistent with the amount of sample required.
    3. Fill the volumetric flask halfway with solvent, swirl to dissolve the sample.
    4. Fill to the mark with solvent, stopper, and shake well to insure good mixing.

NOTE: If extinction coefficients are $10^4$ or greater, desired concentration will be $10^{-4}$M or less. In this case, direct preparation of 5 or 10-mL volumes of solution will not be possible bcause the small masses of sample needed cannot be accurately weighed. For example, only 0.0003g of a sample of MW 300 will be required for 10 mL of 1x $10^{-4}$ M solution. This cannot be weighed on a 4-place analytical balance. You should plan to weigh not less than 20mg of smaple in order to insure accuracy in weighing. The procedure to follow in this case is to prepare 5 mL of solution which is 10 times more concentrated than needed. A 1/2-mL aliquot of this, measured by syringe, can then be diluted to 5 mL and the spectum run. This requires only 9.5 mL of solvent.

2. Extinction coefficients are unknown. If you do not know where and to what extent your compound absorbs—for instance, if it is a new compound—you will have to obtain the spectrum by preparing solutions according to a systematic trial and error procedure.

   1. Prepare a fairly concentrated solution of the sample, say 0.01-0.05 M, in a 5-or 10-mL volumetric flask. Choose the flask size so that the mass of compound required is no less than 20 mg.

      Ex: For a compound of MW 300, the mass required for 5 mL of a 0.01 M solution is calculated as follows:

      ?g = 0.01 moles/L x 0.005 L x 3000 g/mole = 0.0150g = 150 mg.

      Use of a 10mL volumetric flask would require twice as much and would therefore be wasteful.

      For solutions of transition metal complexes, 0.01 M is a good choice because it will allow you to see d-d bands, which have ε values of 1-100 $M^{-1}$ $cm^{-1}$.

   2. Run the spectrum over the vavelength range 900 to 200 nm.

   1. If the least intense absorption bands have absorbance in the range 0.1 to 1, you have chosen a good starting concentration. Depending on the position of the longest wavelength band, reset the long wavelength limit of the spectrometer to eliminate long stretches where there are

no bands, and rerun the spectrum. Pick a convenient limit, like 700 nm, not an inconvenient one, like 721 nm! For example, if the longest wvvelenth band has a maximum at 550 nm, it may be appropriate to start the scan at 700 rather than 900 nm. Maintain this new wavelength range for all subsequent dilution spectra.

2. If the least intense absorption bands are too weak ($A<0.1$), prepare a more concentrated solution and rerun until the conditions in 2a are met.

3. To bring intense absorption bands into the 0-1 absorbance range, dilute the initial solution repeatedly by factors of 2,5, or 10 to give each band in turn the appropriate intensity. Since absorption bands for a compound can have widely different intensities, several dilutions and corresponding spectral scans may have to be made to bring the absorbances of all bands in turn into the 0-1 range. Be sure to stopper and shake the volumetric flask each time you prepare a dilution, to insure uniformity of concentration. If you don't do this, $\varepsilon$ values will not be accurate.

   **Be Sure to Record Each Dilution in Your Notebook.** It is easy to lose track of how many dilutions you have made. Record a dilution as follows:

   I diluted 0.50 mL of solution 1a to 5 mL using $CH_2Cl_2$. Ne concentration is $1.24 \times 10^{-4}$ M. I reran the spectrum. See spectrum 3.31-98-2EAS.

   To repeat, once you have selected a final wavelength range in step 2a, do not change it when running dilution spectra.

   A useful guideline is that EAS bands tend to increase in intensity as gets shorter (energy gets higher). The least intense bands will occur in the near IR and Visible regions (900-400 nm), much more intense bands in the UV (< 400 nm).

4. From the known concentration of the initial solution and

the dilution factors, calculate the concentrations of all dilution solutions and, from the measured absorbances, the extinction coefficients of the bands.

Report data in the format given below:

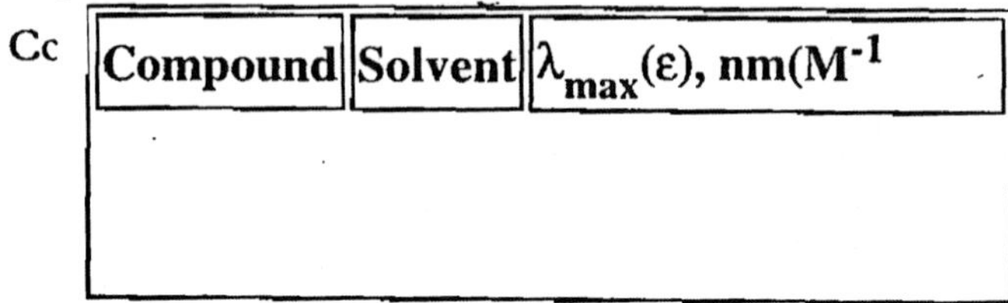

Cc

| Compound | Solvent | $\lambda_{max}(\varepsilon)$, nm($M^{-1}$ |
|---|---|---|
| | | |

NOTE:- A good guideline for coloured samples (i.e., samples which absorb in the visible region) is that the solution should be concentrated enough so that the colour is clearly visible, but of fairly weak intensity in a 1 cm cell. This will usually give absorption bands which fit nicely into the 0-1 absorbance range. However, weaker bands will then be missed.

For the Near IR and UV regions, trial and eror is mandatory.

# 12

# MAGNETISM IN TRANSITION METAL COMPLEXES

Electronic Absorption Spectra of Metal Complexes explains in detail the origin of colour in complexes of the transition metals. We learn that 6 sigma bonding ligands disposed about a metal ion at the vertices of a regular octahedron cause a splitting of the d orbitals of the metal into two sets, one triply degenerate set, n, of non-bonding orbitals ($d_{xy,xz,yz}$), and one doubly degenerate set, $\sigma^\star$, of antibonding orbitals ($d_{z^2, x^2-y^2}$). If these orbitals are partially filled with electrons originally belonging to the metal, and if the ligand field splitting, $\Delta_o$, between the two d orbital sets is such that visible light can cause the transition of an electron from the lower to the upper set, then the complex will be coloured. We will now see that the very interesting and variable magnetic behaviour of transition metals in complexes has its origin in the same basic structural features--split, partially filled d orbitals. With a couple of additional concepts, we can develop a satisfactory explanation of this magnetic behaviour on the basis of the same theory that we used in discussing electronic spectra and colour. We begin with an examination of the various types of magnetic behaviour displayed by matter.

When a piece of matter is placed in a magnetic field, *H* (italic signifies a vector quantity), the mater becomes magnetically polarised; that is a magnetic field is set up in the matter as a result of its presence within the external field, and it has been found experimentally that the strength of the internal field is proportional to the strength of the applied (external) field. We express this mathematically by equation (1) where M is the magnetic polarisation of the matter and $\chi$ is a

$$(K\text{-}1): M = \chi H$$

proportionality constant called the volume magnetic susceptibility. It has been further demonstrated by experiment that $\chi$ may be either negative or positive. Materials for which $\chi$ is small and less than 0 are called diamagnetic materials. Such behaviour is always found for materials that contain no unpaired electrons. Most (but not all) organic compounds qualify as diamagnetic materials, since all their electrons are paired. Diamagnetic behaviour is due to small fields induced in the sample by the applied field that are absent if no external field is present. All materials, regardless of any additional magnetic behaviour they may display, exhibit diamagnetism. Materials for which $\chi$ is greater than 0 are found to contain one or mare unpaired electrons. If $0 < \chi < 1$ (the usual situation), the material is said to be paramagnetic. If on the other hand $\chi > 1$, the material is termed ferromagnetic. Notice that $\chi$ being greater than 1 means that the magnetic field set up in the sample of matter is greater in magnitude than the applied field! This behaviour is exhibited by metallic iron (hence the word ferromagnetic), nickel, and some other metals. Ferromagnetism, however interesting, will not concern us any more at present.

We are interested now in the phenomenon of paramagnetism, which arises whenever a molecule contains unpaired electrons. Oxygen is paramagnetic because it contains two unpaired electrons. $NO_2$ is paramagnetic since it contains an odd number of electrons. (Any substance containing an odd number of electrons must be paramagnetic. Nature usually avoids this situation in compounds of the representative elements, but makes up for it in transition and inner transition elements, where there can be as many as 7 unpaired electrons per molecule.) Organic free radicals are paramagnetic due to the presence of an odd electron (remember the methyl radical, $CH_3$, in free radical halogenation?). As it happens, complexes of most transition metals are paramagnetic as a result of the presence of unpaired electrons in the split d orbitals. We have already encountered an example of this in the complex $Cr(NH_3)_6^{3+}$, which contains 3 unpaired electrons. Consider another example, this time involving $Fe^{III}$, whose electronic configuration is $[Ar]3d^5$ in the absence of ligands. We would expect the free gaseous ion to contain 5 unpaired electrons, as indeed it does--the electrons are distributed in the five degenerate d orbitals, according to the Pauli Exclusion Principle and Humd's Rules, as shown below:

Fig. 12.1

Hund's Rules state that electrons filling a set of degenerate orbitals will fill them so as to maintain their spins parallel for as long as possible. Similarly, the complex $Fe(H_2O)_6^{3+}$, present in strongly acid aqueous solution, contains 5 unpaired electrons. However, the very sable complex $Fe(CN)_6^{3-}$, named hexacyanoferrate (-3), contains only one unpaired electron, even though it also contains Fe(III). We deduce from this that the nature of the ligands must in some way influence the pairing of electrons. But how? Let's call on what we have learned about the splitting of the d orbitals by the ligands. Figure 12.2 shows the situation in items of an energy level diagram.

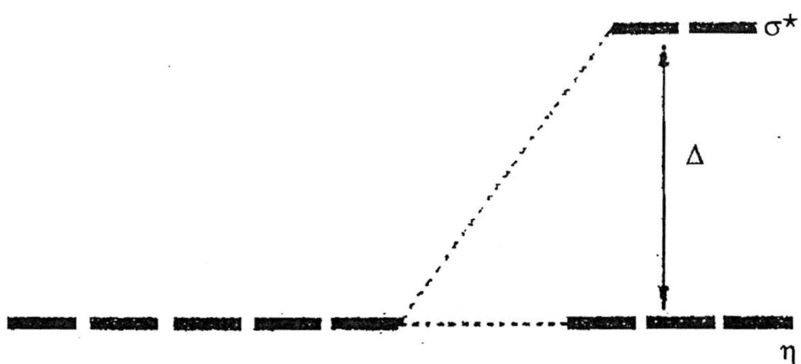


**Figure 12.2**

In the complex, 5 electrons must distribute themselves among the d orbitals, which as a result of the presence of 6 ligands are no longer all degenerate. There is no ambiguity about where the first three electrons will go--one electron will enter each of the three degenerate orbitals in the n set. The fourth electron, however, is faced with a choice: it can either pair up with one of the electrons in a lower orbital, requiring the expenditure of an amount of energy, P, called the pairing energy; or it can occupy one of the orbitals in the uppor doubly degenerate set at the expense of the energy. $\Delta_o$, since the upper set, σ*, is less stable by than the lower set, *n*. The electron will take the option which requires the expenditure of the least energy. If $\Delta_o < P$, it will occupy one of the σ* orbitals. $\Delta_o > P$, the electron will pair up in *n*. The fifth electron will be faced with the same choice, and will make the same decision. Two situations are therefore possible in octahedral complexes of $Fe^{III}$.

σ*

In one case, five unpaired electrons are present. This is called the high spin (HS) case and must correspond to the situation in $Fe(H_2O)_6^{3+}$. In the second case, called the low spin (LS) case, only one unpaired electron is present--the maximum possible amount of electron pairing has occurred. This is the situation which is $Fe(CN)_6^{3-}$. We conclude, then, that when $H_2O$ is the ligand, $\Delta_o < P$ and that when CN- is the ligand, $\Delta_o > P$ (P remains essentially the same for a given metal ion, regardless of ligand, and can be obtained from spectroscopic measurements of the free metal ion, in this case $Fe^{III}$.) We call water a relatively "weak-field ligand" and cyanide a "strong-field ligand."

Any ion having as few as 4 or as many as 7 d electrons can exhibit either high- or low spin behaviour in an octahedral complex. You should work out the numbers of unpaired electrons expected in octahedral complexes of metal ions with configurations d1 to d9 to convince yourself of this. The theory that we have developed above explains beautifully most aspects of the magnetic behavior of transition metal complexes, the exceptions being the more subtle aspects that we will avoid for the time being. Let's turn now to the relationship between the number of unpaired electrons possessed by a molecule and its behaviour in a magnetic field.

There are two sources of magnetic behaviour in matter: 1) orbital motion of electrons; 2) spin of electrons. We will deal with spin motion only now, since it is the most important source of magnetic behaviour in complexes of transition metals. Pictured below is an electron spinning (rotating) about its own axis.

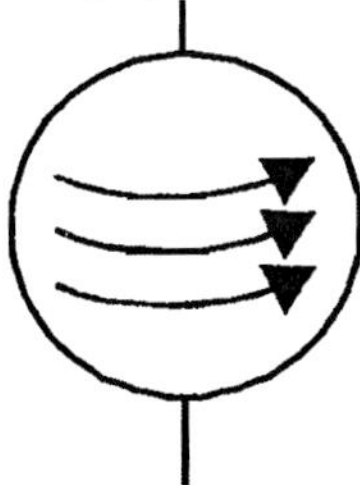

This motion is analogous to the rotation of the earth about its axis. Since the electron is a charged particle, this rotational motion constitutes an electric current. To see this more clearly, mentally replace the electron with a loop of wire in which a current is flowing:

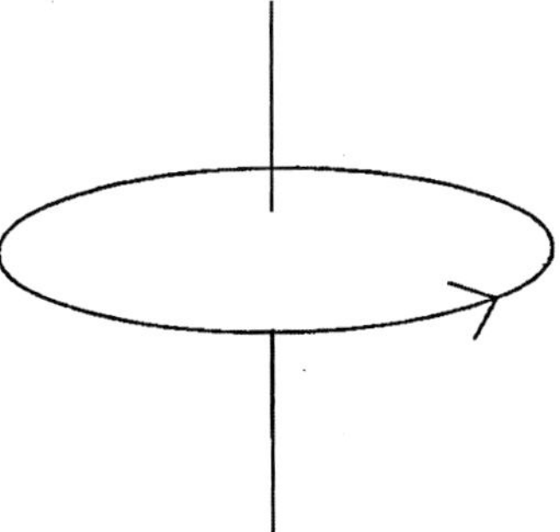

Recall from your study of electricity and magnetism in physics, that a flow of current always generates a magnetic field. When the current is flowing in a loop, the direction of the magnetic field is perpendicular to the plane of the loop. Thus.

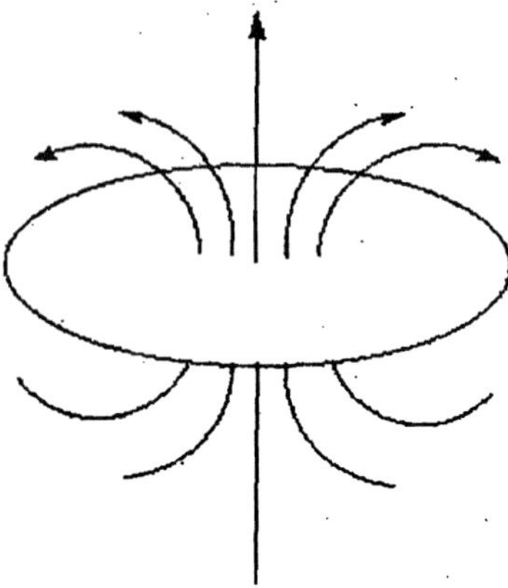

The spin of the electron about its axis, since it is an electric current, similarly generates a magnetic field parallel to the axis of rotation. This magnetic field is called the spin magnetic moment of the electron, and is given the symbol $\mu$s. The arrow over the symbol indicates that the magnetic moment is a vector quantity. Now rotational motion of any kind always generates angular momentum, which is also a vector parallel to the axis of rotation. The magnetic moment and the angular momentum are therefore colinear vectors. Furthermore, their magnitudes are directly proportional. This is indicated in the following equation.

$$\text{(K-2)}: \mu = \gamma L$$

where $L$ = angular momentum and $\gamma$ is the proportionality constant relating magnetic moment and angular momentum. When a paramagnetic sample is placed in an external magnetic field, the individual spin magnetic moments of the unpaired electrons all line up with the field, just as iron filings line up along the magnetic lines of flux generated by a bar magnet. Their vector sum is the magnetic polarisation defined by equation (1). Thus we see that magnetic polarisation, which is a macroscopic property, is related to individual spin magnetic moments, which are microscopic properties of the system.

It can be shown that the magnetic moment of an individual ion in a sample is related to the number of unpaired electrons on the ion by the following equation.

(K-3): $\mu s=[n(n+2)]^{1/2}$ Bohr magnetons

The Bohr magneton is a convenient unit for expressing magnetic moments, and is defined in terms of fundamental constants as 1 BM=eh/4πmc. Here, *e* = the charge on the electron, *h* = Planck's constant, *m* = the mass of the electron, and *c* = the speed of light, and, in equation (K-3), *n* = the number of unpaired electrons per ion. We can therefore calculate the number of unpaired electrons per molecule of sample if we can measure the magnetic moment. In practice, we can relatively easily measure the molar magnetic susceptibility of a material, which is then related to the magnetic moment by equation (4).

# 13

# CHELATION

Chemical reaction or process involving chelate ring formation and characterised by multiple coordinate bonding between two or more of the electron-pair-donor groups of a multidentate ligand and an electron-pair-acceptor metal ion. The multidentate ligand is usually called a chelating agent, and the product is known as a metal chelate compound or metal chelate complex. Metal chelate chemistry i a subdivision of coordination chemistry and is characterised by the special properties resulting from the utilisation of ligands possessing bridged donor groups, two or more of which coordinate simultaneously to a metal ion. See also: Coordination chemistry Ethylenediamine, $H_2NCH_2CH_2NH_2$, is a good example of a bidentate chelating agent consisting of two amino donor groups joined to each other by a two-carbon bridge. The coordination of both nitrogen atoms to the same metal ion would result in the formation of a five-membered chelate ring. If a chelating agent has three groups capable of attaching to a metal ion, as in diethylenetriamine, $NH_2CH_2CH_2NHCH_2CH_2NH_2$, it is tridentate (terdentate); if four, tetradentate (quadridentate); five, pentadentate (quinquidentate); six, hexadentate (sexadentate); and so on. In general, these chelating agents may be designated as multidentate or polydentate ligands. All chelating agents must be at least bidentate; tridentate agents give fused rings. An example of a nonchelated complex and two chelated complexes of the Cd(II) ion are illustrated in Fig. 13.1. In aqueous solution, metal ions are completely solvated, or hydrated, to give an aquo complex, as indicated for the Cd(II) ion in. Fig.13.1. Thus formation of a complex of a unidentate ligand involves the replacement of a water molecule by the unidentate donor group. Two water molecules are replaced by a single molecule of a bidentate ligand; three water molecules are replaced by a molecule of a terdentate ligand, and so on.

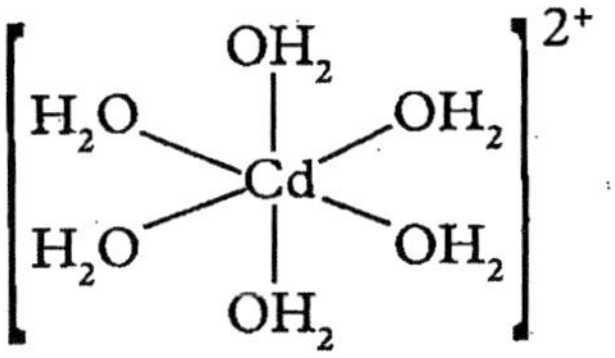

Aquo cadmium (II) ion

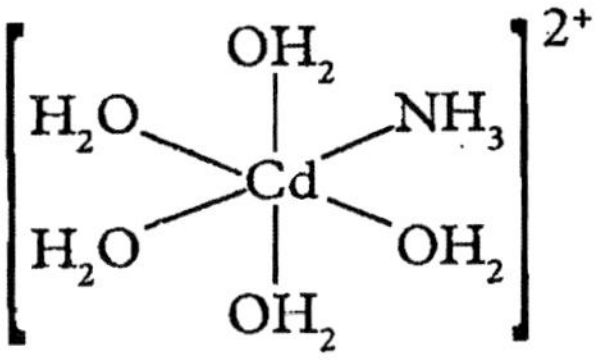

1:1 Cadmium (II)-complex ammonia.

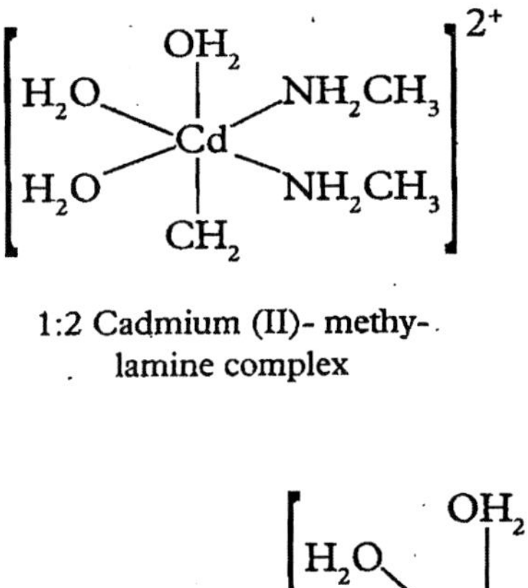

1:2 Cadmium (II)- methy-lamine complex

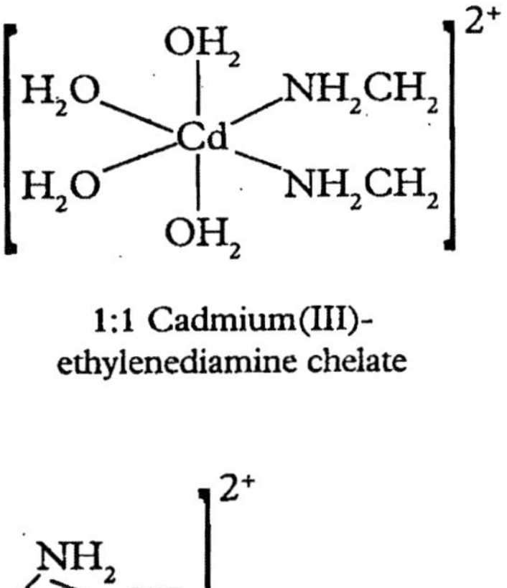

1:1 Cadmium(III)-ethylenediamine chelate

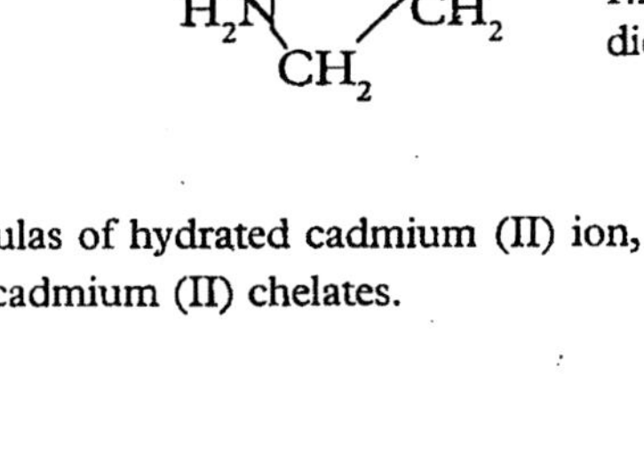

1:2 Cadmium (II)-diethylenetriamine chelate

Fig.13.1: Formulas of hydrated cadmium (II) ion, two cadmium (II) complexes, and two cadmium (II) chelates.

Many of the functional groups of both synthetic and naturally occurring organic compounds can form coordinate bonds to metal ions, producing metal-organic complexes or chelates, many of which are biologically active. Thus chelate compounds are frequently found in an interdisciplinary field of science called bioinorganic chemistry. The biological significance of chelates can be readily recognised if one notes that a large number of biologically important compounds are either metal chelates or chelating agents. This list includes the alpha amino acids, peptides, proteins, enzymes, porphyrins (such as hemoglobin), corrins (such as vitamin $B_{12}$), catechols, hydroxypolycarboxylic acids (such as citric acid), ascorbic acid (vitamin C), polyphosphates, nucleosides and other genetic compounds, pyridoxal phosphate (vitamin $B_6$), and sugars. The ubiquitous green plant pigment, chlorophyll, is a magnesium chelate of a tetradentate ligand formed from a modified porphin compound, and similarly the oxygen transport heme of red blood cells contains an Fe(II) chelate of the type illustrated in Fig. 13.2. See also: Bioinorganic chemistry; Organometallic compound

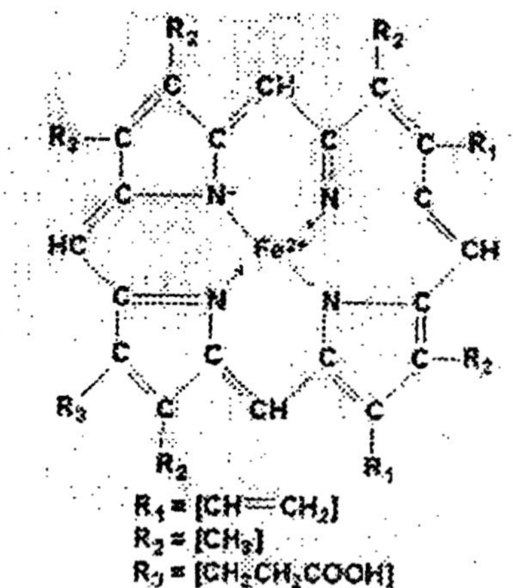


Fig. 13.2 : Heme, a tetradentate chelate of iron (II)

A rapidly growing body of experimental evidence indicates taht chelation may be important in the pharmacological action of many drugs. The use of chelating agents to remove certain toxic cations such as lead and plutonium from the body is now widely recognised in medical practice. Intensive research has been undertaken to either develop or discover an effective synthetic or natural chelating agent for the removal of iron deposits in the body that result from certain hereditary metabolic disorders.

## Applications

The ability of chelating agents to reduce the chemical activity of metal ions has found extensive application in many areas of science and industry.

Ethylenediaminetetraacetic acid (EDTA), a hexadentate chelating agent (Fig. 13.3), has been employed commercially for water softening, boiler scale removal, industrial cleaning, soil metal micronutrient transport, and food preservation. Nitrilotriacetic acid (NTA) is a tetradentate chelating agent (Fig. 13.4) which, because of lower cost, has taken over some of the commercial applications of EDTA. Chelating agents of related type have been used in biological systems to produce metal-ion buffers. By selection of the appropriate chelating agent, the free metal-ion concentration can be maintained at a very low and constant

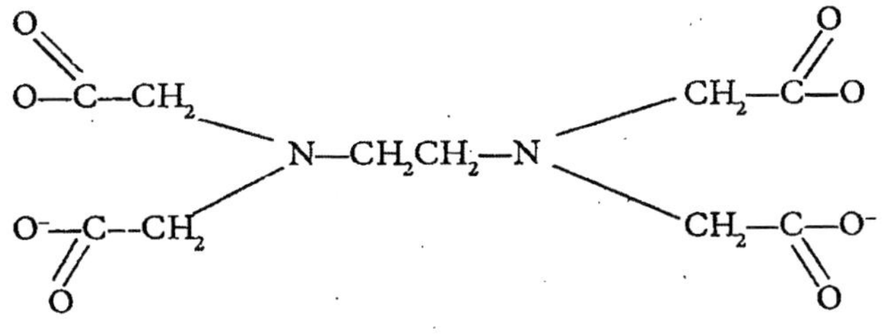

O=C(O)—$CH_2$      $CH_2$—C(=O)—O

N—$CH_2CH_2$—N

$O^-$—C(=O)—$CH_2$      $CH_2$—C(=O)—$O^-$

**Fig. 13.3:** Structural formula of anion of EDTA, a sexadentate ligand.

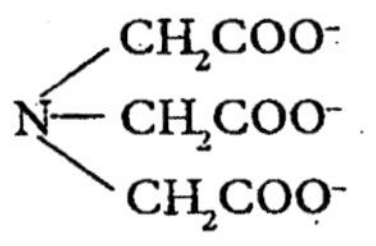

N—$CH_2COO^-$, $CH_2COO^-$, $CH_2COO^-$

**Fig 13.4:** Structural formula of NTA anion, a quadridentate ligand.

concentration level, just as a relatively constant pH can be maintained through the use of a conventional hydrogen-ion buffer system. Furthermore, the colours of certain chelating agents are sensitive to metal-ion concentration in a manner completely analogous to the pH-dependent colour changes observed with acid-base indicators; such chelating agents serve as metal-ion indicators in analytical chemistry. The solubility of many chelating agents and metal chelates in organic solvents permits their use in solvent extraction of aqueous solutions for the separation or analysis of metal ions.

Many commercially important dyes and pigments, such as copper phthalocyanines, are chelate compounds. Humic and fulvic acids are plant degradation products in lake and seawater sediments that have been suggested as important chelating agents which regulate metal-ion balance in natural waters. By virtue of its abundance, low toxicity, low cost, and good chelating tendencies for metal ions that produce water hardness, the tripolyphosphate ion (as its sodium salt) is used in large quantities as a builder in synthetic detergents. Both synthetic ion exchangers and the mineral zeolites are chelating ion-exchange resins which are used in analytical and water-softening applications. As final examples, less conventional chelating agents are the multidentate, cyclic ligands, termed collectively crown ethers, which are particularly suited for the complexation of the alkali and alkaline-earth metals.

## Stabilities of Metal Chelates in Solution

One of the most striking properties of chelate ring compounds is their unusual thermodynamic and thermal stability. In this respect, they resemble the aromatic rings of organic chemistry. For example, in reaction (1), β-diketones in the enol form can lose a hydrogen ion and coordinate with a metal cation to give a six membered ring of unusual thermal stability.

Beryllium acetylacetonate boils without decomposition at 270°C (518°F), and G.T. Morgan reported that scandium acetylacetonate, $Sc(acac)_3$, shows very little decomposition at

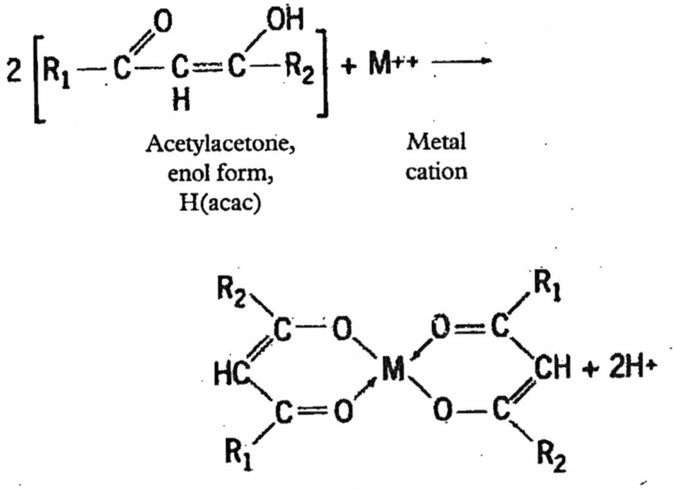

$$2\left[R_1-\overset{\overset{O}{\|}}{C}-\underset{H}{C}=\overset{\overset{OH}{|}}{C}-R_2\right] + M^{++} \longrightarrow$$

Acetylacetone, enol form, H(acac)

Metal cation

$$M(acac)_2 + 2H^+ \quad (1)$$

Metal acetylacetonate, $M(acac)_2$

370°C (698°F). This remarkable stability contrasts sharply with the very low stability of coordination compounds containing simpler monodentate ketones, such as acetone.

Because of enhanced thermodynamic stability in solution, chelating agents may greatly alter the behaviour of metal ions. The very insoluble compound, ferric hydroxide, will dissolve in a strongly alkaline solution of triethanol amine, $N(CH_2CH_2OH)_3$. Alternatively, the concentration of the feric ion can be made vanishingly small at pH 2 by the addition of an equimolar amount of bis(orthohydroxybenxyl) ethylenediamine-*N,N'*-diacetic acid (HBED; Fig.13.5).

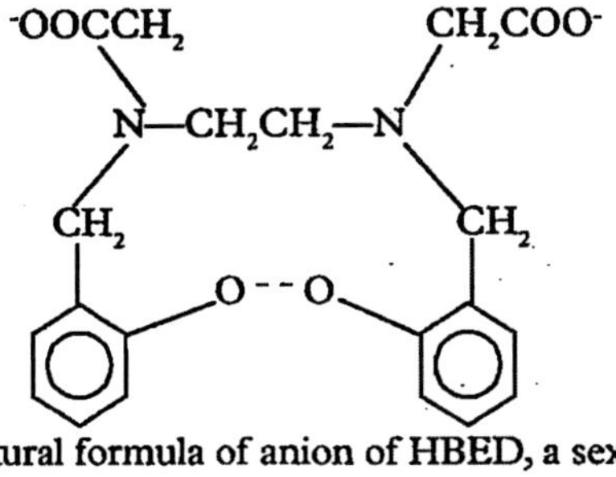

$^{-}OOCCH_2$ — N — $CH_2CH_2$ — N — $CH_2COO^{-}$ (each N bearing $CH_2$ linked to a phenolate O)

Fig. 13.5: Structural formula of anion of HBED, a sexadentate ligand.

Since about 1940, both theoretical and practical considerations have focused attention on the factors which contribute to chelate stability. It is convenient to list such factors under three headings: (1) the nature of the metal cation, (2) the nature of the ligand, and (3) the formation of the chelate ring. It should be emphasised that these factors operate together, and their separation is somewhat artificial, but helpful for discussion purposes.

## Role of Metal in Chelate Stability

Since nitrogen, oxygen, and sulphur serve as the electron donor atoms in a majority of chelating agents, it is of interest to seek a relationship between the donor atom and the type of metal acceptor atom with which it combines. A large majority of the chelates of $Li^+$ , $Na^+$, $K^+$, $Rb^+$, $Cs^+$, $Mg^{2+}$, $Ca^{2+}$, $Sr^{2+}$, $Ba^{2+}$, $Al^{3+}$, $Ga^{3+}$, $In^{3+}$, $Tl^{3+}$, $Ti^{4+}$, $Zr^{4+}$, $Th^{4+}$, $Si^{4+}$, $Ge^{4+}$, and $Sn^{4+}$, contain oxygen as at least one of the donor atoms. It may be furnished as an acid, alcohol, ether, ketone, or other group. These ions coordinate less frequently through two nitrogen or sulphur atoms. Cations of other metals such as vanadium, niobium, tantalum, molybdenum, and uranium, and the cations $Be^{2+}$, $Al^{3+}$, and $Fe^{3+}$, show a preference for oxygen as the donor atom, but they may coordinate through nitrogen, sulphur, or phosphorus under special conditions. $Cr^{3+}$, $Fe^{2+}$, and the platinum metals show increasing preference for coordination through nitrogen as opposed to oxygen, while $Cu^+$, $Zn^{2+}$, $Ag^+$, $Au^+$, $Cu^{2+}$, $Cd^{2+}$, $Hg^{2+}$, $V^{2+}$, $Co^{3+}$, and $Ni^{2+}$, show a marked preference for nitrogen and sulphur as the donor atoms. The ions of the last group retain the ability to coordinate with oxygen in even greater degree than do the ions of the first group, but their tendency to form bonds through nitrogen is so great that it exceeds their oxygen binding tendency.

It must be recognised that broad generalisations such as these have many exceptions, particularly in intermediate regions. On the other hand, such generalisations indicate clearly that attempts to arrange elements in the order of their chelating ability can be of significance only when cations of comparable type are selected. Thus, the stabilities of the alkali-metal, the alkaline-earth, and the rare-earth chetales decrease as the charge on the cation decreases or as the size of the cation increases. For example, the chelates of the alkaline-earth metal ions become less stable as the metal ion becomes larger (if the number of chelate rings remains the same), in the order $Mg^{2+}$, $Ca^{2+}$, $Sr^{2+}$, $Ba^{2+}$, $Ra^{2+}$. The relationship between ion size and chelate stability is of major importance in the separation of the rare-earth and transuranium elements by ion-exchange processes. The selectivity of the ion-exchange column is increased by the use of appropriate chelating agents in the eluting solution.

Stability sequences established for other metal ions are somewhat less satisfactory. Metal chelates of several substituted$^{\beta}$ -diketones decrease in stability in the order:

$Hg^{2+} > (Cu^{2+}, Be^{2+}) > Ni^{2+} > Co^{2+} > Zn^{2+} > Pb^{2+} > Mn^{2+} > Cd^{2+} > Mg^{2+} > Ca^{2+} > Sr^{2+} > Ba^{2+}$.

If one restricts stability comparisons to bivalent metals of the first transition series, the following order is obtained: $Zn^{2+} < Cu^{2+} > Ni^{2+} > Co^{2+} > Fe^{2+} > Mn^{2+}$. This latter listing of stabilities appears to be valid for a large variety of chelating ligands. Lower valence states such as Ir(I) and Rh(I) are effectively coordinated by chelating ligands containing trivalent phosphorus or trivalent arsenic donor groups. For example, recently synthetic coordination chemists have synthesised a series of unusual chelating agents containing trivalent phosphorus, analogous to polyamines, an example of which is illustrated in Fig. 13.6.

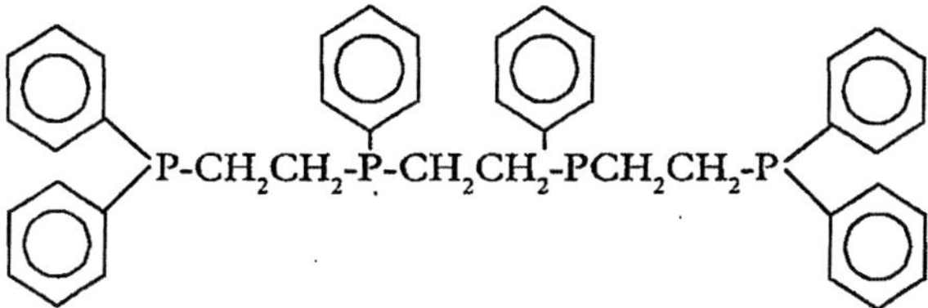


Fig. 13.6 : "Tetraphos," a quadridentate ligand.

General principles of selective coordination of metal ions by various types of donor atoms have now been worked out, and are described through concepts such as the principles of hard and soft acids and bases, and type A and B character of metal ions.

These qualitative principles are based on well-known laws of ionic attraction and polarisabilities of atoms, ions, or molecular groups, as well as on general principles of molecular orbital theory.

## Role of Ligand in Chelate Stability

Two general types of groups give rise to coordinate bonds between ligands and metal. These are (1) primary acid groups in which the matal ion can replace hydrogen ions and (2) neutral groups which contain an atom with a free electron pair suitable for bond formation. If two groups from either class 1 or 2, or from both classes, are present in the same molecule in such positions that both groups can form bonds with the same metal ion, a chelate ring may be formed. For example, as shown in Fig.13.7, in oxalic acid two groups of type 1 are present; in ethylenediamine two groups of type 2 are present; glycine possesses one of each type; and pyridoxylidine-glycine (the Schiff base of glycine and vitamin $B_6$) possesses a carboxylate (type 1), an aromatic phenolate (type 1), and an imino group (type 2) available for chelate formation around a metal ion.

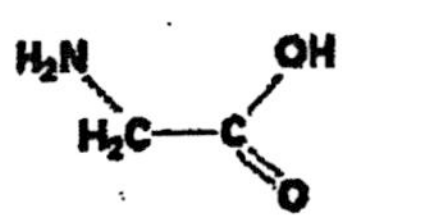

Oxalic acid; two type 1 (negative carboxylate) donor groups

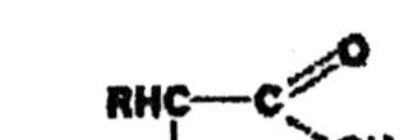

Ethylenediamine: two type 2 (neutral amino) donor groups

Glycine; one type 1 and one type 2 donor group

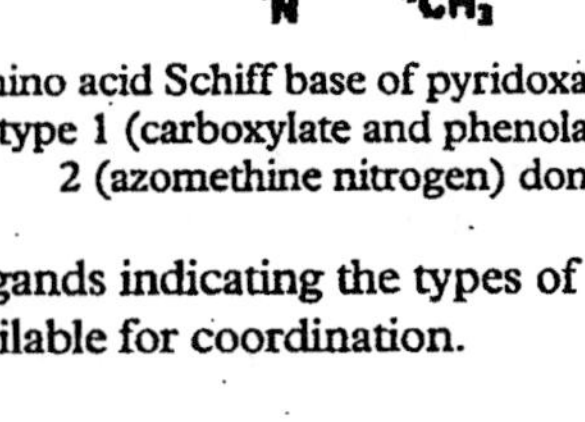

Amino acid Schiff base of pyridoxal (vitamine $B_6$); two type 1 (carboxylate and phenolate) and one type 2 (azomethine nitrogen) donor group

Fig. 13.7: Chelating ligands indicating the types of donor groups available for coordination.

In general, anything which increases the localisation of negative charge on the donor atom increases its ability to coördinate to a metal atom. Since a hydrogen ion is bound to a ligand by an electron pair in groups of type 1; an increase in electron density on the donor atom will increase the ability of the donor to bind either hydrogen ion or metal cation. The ability of a ligand to bind hydrogen ion is frequently referred to as its basic strength. It is surprising then that, for ligands of rather similar type, an increase in ligand basic strength implies an increase in its metal-chelating ability. A number of researchers have indicated this relationship by plotting the log of the equilibrium constant for the process represented by Eq. (2) against the log of the equilibrium constant forthe process of chelate dissociation shown by Eq. (3) $L^-$ is the chelating

$$H^+ + L^- \rightleftharpoons HL \qquad K_1 = \frac{[HL]}{[H+][L-]} \qquad (2)$$

$$M^{n+} + L^- \rightleftharpoons M^{(n-1)+} \qquad K_2 = \frac{[ML^{(n-1)+}]}{[M^{n+}][L^-]} \qquad (3)$$

anion, such as the acetylacetonate anion,

$$\begin{array}{c} CH_3\text{—}C\text{—}CH = C\text{—}CH_3 \\ \quad \| \qquad\quad \| \\ \quad O \qquad -O \end{array}$$

The constant $K_1$ is the protonation constant (its reciprocal is the acid dissociation constant), and $K_2$ is designated the sability constant of the metal chelate. For the organic chemist, the analogy between the hydrogen cation and the metal cation is even more clearly drawn. Rings formed by hydrogen bonding are referred to as chelates; thus, formic acid dimerises through hydrogen-bond chelation as shown in Fig. 13.8. The high volatility of *o*-nitrophenol compared with the much lower volatility of its meta or para isomers (Fig. 13.8) can only be explained in terms of intramolecular versus intermolecular hydrogen bonding. The properties of salicylaldehyde, enhanced enolization in acetoacetic ester, and many other organic compunds are altered by internal chelate-ring formation involving hydrogen bonds. See also: Hydrogen bond.

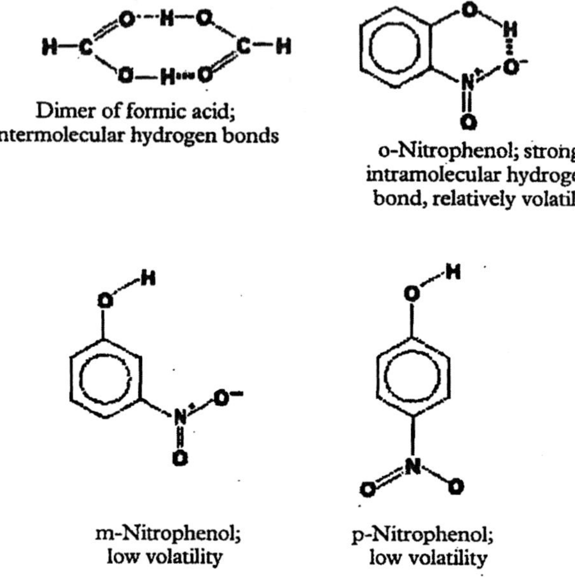


Fig. 13.8: Compounds forming intramolecular and intermolecular hydrogen bonds.

The role or ligand structure on chelate stability is illustrated by studies which have been conducted on compounds of the type shown by Fig. 13.9, where A represents an electron-attracting group. In general, it was found that with an increase in the electron-attracting power of group A, electrons were pulled away from the nitrogen atom, resulting in both lower base strength and lower chelating ability for the ligand. As A is changed successively through the groups *shown below,* chelate stability increases in the order:

Similar studies on substitute *β-diketone chelates* of the type showed that, if $R_1$ were changed from a methyl group to an electron-withdrawing trifluoromethyl group, the stability of the resulting chelate is greatly decreased. In general, all molecular charge effects which can be invoked to shift charge in an organic molecule, such as inductive and resonance effects, will influence chelate stability. Thus the principles governing charge distribution and bond hybridization in organic chemistry are useful in working out the relationships between ligand structure and chelate stability.

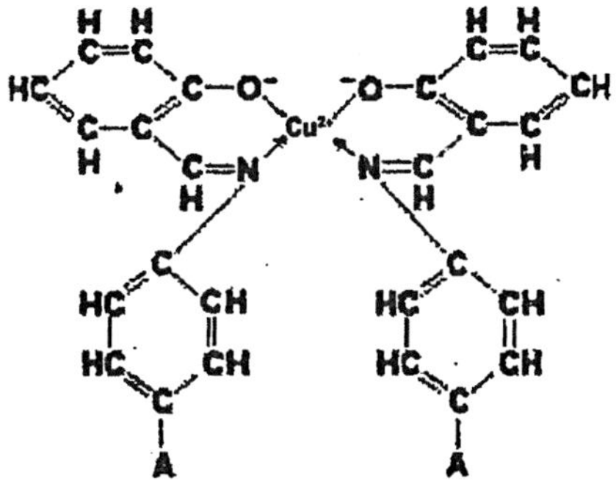

Fig. 13.9: Structure of a chelated copper compound.

## Role of Ring Closure in Chelate Stability

The stability factors discussed above are applicable to coordination compounds generally, not to chelates alone. On the other hand, a number of stability factors may be considered to apply uniquely to chelates because of their ring structure. The most obvious variable in this category is ring size, a factor which is uniquely determined by the position of the donor atoms in the chelating ligand. When the groups are present in such a position as to form a five or six-membered ring, the resulting complex is the most stable although four-, severn-, eight-membered, and even larger rings are known. Examples of these would be found among biological ligands as well as in ion exchange resins. The existence of three-membered rings has not been established. Hydrazine, $H_2NNH_2$, which might in theory form a three-membered chelate ring, appears to be monodentate. There is some evidence for intermediate structures of metal-oxygen complexes which may be considered three-memberd chelate rings. Such compounds may be important reaction intermediates but are generally unstable and present in relatively low concentrations. The four-membered chelate rings are frequently strained. Examples of four-membered chelate rings are copper(II)-carboxylate complexes, and the aluminum chloride dimer (Fig. 13.10). While five-membered rings are very common and are formed preferentially by saturated organic ligands, ligands containing two double bounds tend to form six-membered structures. If only one double bond is present, five- or six-membered rings may form; five-membered saturated rings are illustrated in Fig. 13.10 by ethylene-diamine-metal chelates, and the conjugated six-membered rigns by the metal acetylacetonates.

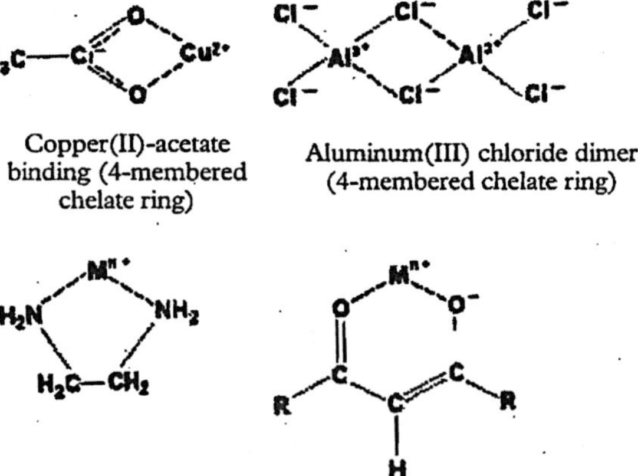


**Fig. 13.10: Metal chelates containing four-, five-, and six-membered rings.**

Rings of seven or more members are comparatively uncommon, but their existence is well established. As the length of the chain between the two donor atoms increases, so does the tendency of the ligand to form polymetallic complexes. Under such circumstances, the two donor atoms on the same chelate molecule coordinate with different metal atoms rather than with one; thus, a polymeric chain, $M^+$ - $NH_2$ $CH_2CH_2CH_2CH_2NH_2$-$M^+$, may result instead of a ring structure.

The fact that chelate complexes are usually more stable than comparable nonchelate structures has been called the chelate effect. This effect is partly attributable to the fact that simultaneous rupture of both bonds holding the ligand to the metal is highly improbable, and if only one bond breaks there is a high probability that the broken bond will reform before the second bond is reptured. As the chain length between the two donor atoms increases, the chance for reformation of the broken bond declines; thus, large rings usually show a decrease in stability. On the other hand, in fused ring systems, formed by polydentate ligands such as ethylenediaminetetraacetic acid, the probability that at least one bond will reform before all bonds are ruptured results in increased complex stability. When the bonding atoms are rigidly positioned around the metal by the organic framework, as in the porphins, the resulting increase in stability is extremely high. It has been reported that the copper phthalocyanine complex, with a completely interlocked ring system, is stable in the vapour phase near 500°C (930°F).

Chelate compounds are differentiated from thier nonchelate analogs by several properties besides high stability. Although not all chelates are volatile, the existence of low-boiling metal acetylacetonates and related structures in noteworthy. If the coordination number of the metal cation for the oxygen atoms of the acetylacetone (that is, the number of nearest oxygens around the cation) is equal to twice the ionic charge of the cation, the resulting acetylacetonate is volatile; thus, beryllium with a charge of 2 and a coordination number of 4 forms an acetylacetonate which boils at 270°C (518°F); aluminum with a charge of 3 and a coordination number of 6 forms an acetylacetonate which boils at 314°C (597°F). If the coordination number of the central cation is less than twice the ionic charge, less volatile saltlike complexes are formed.

Isomerism of all types, so important in organic chemistry, is of major concern in chelation, particularly to the biochemist, since desired bilogical properties are frequently restricted to a particular chelate isomer. Ring formation may result in optical activity where analogous nonchelate structures are inactive. Thus, the ethylenediamine chelate structures shown in Fig. 13.11 are optical isomers, whereas the analogous methylamine complexes represented in Fig. 13.12 are optically inactive.

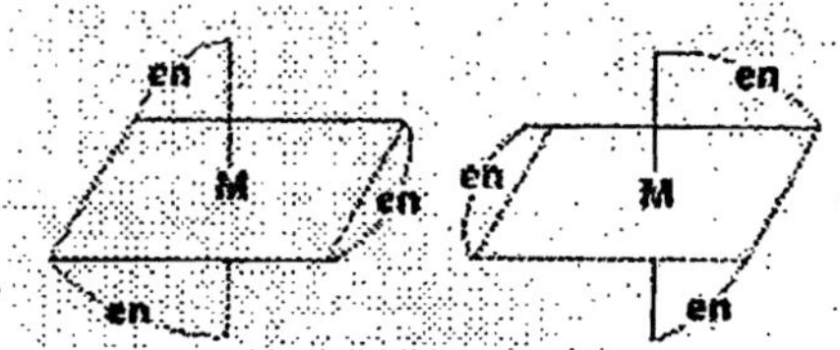


Fig. 13.11: Optical isomers of chelate complexes.

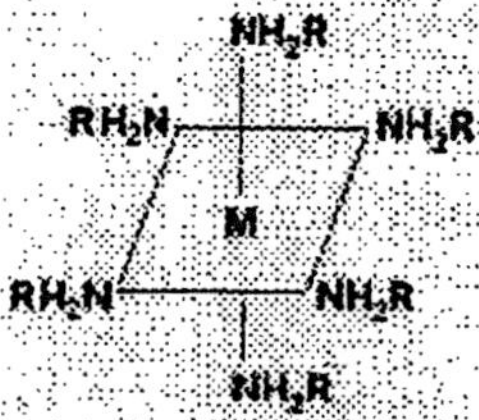


Fig. 13.12: Formula for an optically inactive nonchelate.

# 14

# METAL CARBONYLS

Carbon monoxide is an excellent example of a $\pi$-acceptor ligand. In this cases it is the carbonyl $\pi^*$ orbitals which are of the correct symmetry to interact. There are two types of interaction to consider. The first is a $\sigma$-donor interaction from the CO carbon one pair into an empty metal orbital. Looked at simplistically the triple bond of CO is made up from a $\sigma$ bond and two $\pi$ bonds. The $\pi$ orbitals of CO are filled but it is the *empty* $\pi^*$ orbitals which are of interest here. For convenience the situation is discussed here just for an octahedral complex. The arguments are, however, similar for other geometries. The metal $t_{2g}$ orbital (the $d_{xy}$, $d_{xz}$, and $d_{yz}$ orbitals) of the octahedral metal complex are normally filled in this type of complex. The $\pi^*$ orbitals are of the correct symmetry to overlap with the metal $t_{2g}$ orbitals. This is shown for a single CO ligand in Fig. 14.2. There is an exactly equivalent interaction involving the second $\pi^*$ orbital at right angles to that shown. The six CO ligands between them possess twelve $\pi^*$ orbitals. Again, strictly, the complex should be considered as a whole and the reader is left to construct a diagram for carbonyl bonding analogous to Fig 14.1 to reflect this.

In this situation, the metal $t_{2g}$ orbitals would normally be filled. The interaction between the metal $t_{2g}$ orbitals and linear combinations of the CO $\pi^*$ orbitals effectively means that there is a flow of electron density from the metal to the ligand (Fig. 14.3). The donation of electrons from the metal to the ligand is referred to as *'back-bonding'* since the direction of electron transfer

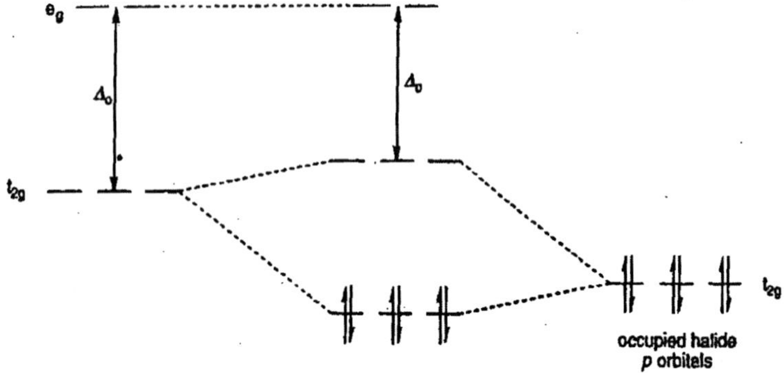


Fig. 14.1: The interaction between empty metal $t_{2g}$ orbitals and filled halide *p* orbitals in an octahedral environment.

(M→L) is the opposite to that normally seen (L→M). The sysmmetry of the overlap is clearly π-type, hence the term π back-bonding. Recall the definitions of the terms *Lewis acid* and *Lewis base* which involve the terms '*electron acceptor*' and '*electron donor*' respectively. Therefore the ligand CO is quite reasonably referred to as a 'π-acid' as well as a 'σ-base'. To correspond with this, halides are π-bases as well as σ-bases.

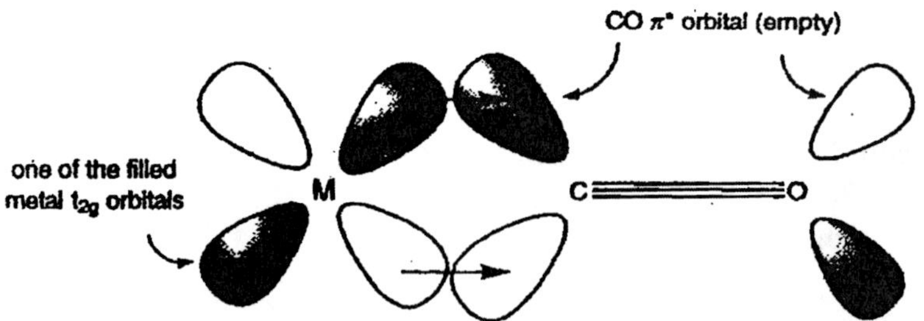


Fig. 14.2: One of the π-bonding contributions in a M—CO bond.

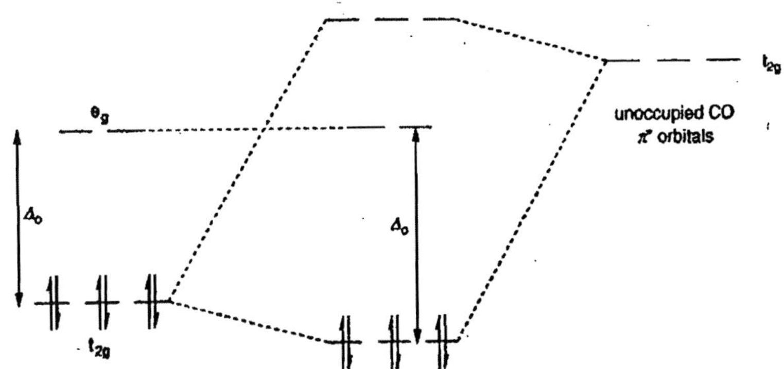


Fig. 14.3: The interaction of filled metal $t_{2g}$ and vacant CO $\pi^*$ orbitals.

To sum up, *carbon monoxide acts as a σ-donor and a π-acceptor.* When the bonding situation is such that electrons are transferred in one direction and other electrons accepted in the reverse direction, the bonding is said to be synegistic, (*synergy,* Gr. synergia, n. combined or coordinated action). The bonding is cooperative in the sense that electrons transferred in one direction would lead to an unacceptable charge build up at the other centre, but for the removal of some electron density in the reverse direction, and so on. Up to a point the σ-interaction strengthens the π-interaction, and *vice versa.*

Overall, there is only a small dipole moment associated with the M—C interaction, suggesting approximate electroneutrality. However, the effect of the electronegative oxygen atom is to cause a small charge imbalance between carbon, which becomes slightly positively charged, ($\delta^+$) and oxygen which becomes slightly negatively charged ($\delta^-$). This renders the carbon atom somewhat prone to attack by nucleophiles (such as hydride donors) and the oxygen by electrophiles (such as $AlCl_3$).

The effect of the orbital interactions illustrated in Fig. 14.3 upon the metal $t_{2g}$ orbitals is to produce a set of bonding orbitals with the predominant appearance of metal $t_{2g}$ orbitals but *lower* in energy. In the $d^6$ situation, these orbitals are filled and since the energy of these electrons drops, the overall effect is to increase the total bonding of the system. Note that in the σ-bonding only case, the metal $t_{2g}$ orbitals are nonbinding but for a complex with π-acceptor ligands are bonding. The π-interaction has no effect upon the $e_g$ orbitals since there are no ligand orbital combinations with $e_g$ symmetry. The net effect of a π-acceptor ligand is therefore to increase the splitting between the $e_g$ and $t_{2g}$ orbitals, that is, to *increase* Δ°.

## Evidence for π-acceptor Properties of CO

Multiple bonds between elements tend to shorten the internuclear distance. Thus a C—C bond is about 154 pm in length whereas a C=C bond is 134 pm. The back bonding phenomenon for metal carbonyl complexes corresponds to an increase in bond order between the metal and the carbonyl carbon atom. Therefore the metal—carbon bond should be shorter than a M—C single bond. The X-ray crystal structures of metal carbonyl complexes such as $[Cr(CO)_3 \text{ (dien)}]$ (Fig. 14.4) provides evidence for this bond shortening. Each of the nitrogen atoms in this complex is $sp^3$ hybridized and $sp^3$ hybridized nitrogen has an atomic radius of 70 pm. Each carbonyl carbon is $sp$ hybridized and has exactly the same atomic radius as $sp^3$ nitrogen. However although all the ligand atoms are the same size, the chromium-carbon bond lengths are

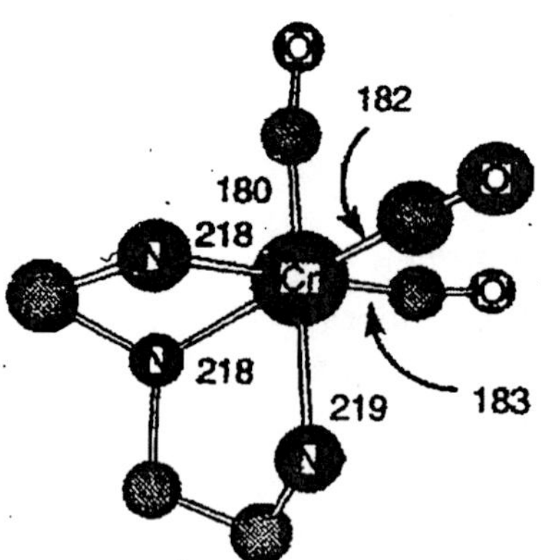


Fig. 14.4 : The solid state structure of $[Cr(CO)_3 \text{ (dien)}]$. Bond lengths expressed in pm.

all somewhat shorter than the chromium-nitrogen bond lengths. Assuming the chromium is spherical, this is good evidence for multiple bond character in metal-carbonyl interactions. Similar arguments based upon M—L bond lengths apply to other π-acceptor ligands.

## Dinitrogen Complexes

Dinitrogen, $N_2$, is also isoelectronic with CO. As such, one might expect there to be many $N_2$ complexes in the literature. In practice, there are relatively few. The relative energies of its orbitals renders $N_2$ a weaker σ-donor than CO, as well as a weaker π-acceptor. The first $N_2$ complex was synthesised in 1965 from the reaction of aqueous $RuCl_3$ with hydrazine (Fig. 14.5). Sometimes, $N_2$ can act as a bridging ligand between two metals. Other examples of dinitrogen complexes are shown in Fig. 14.6.

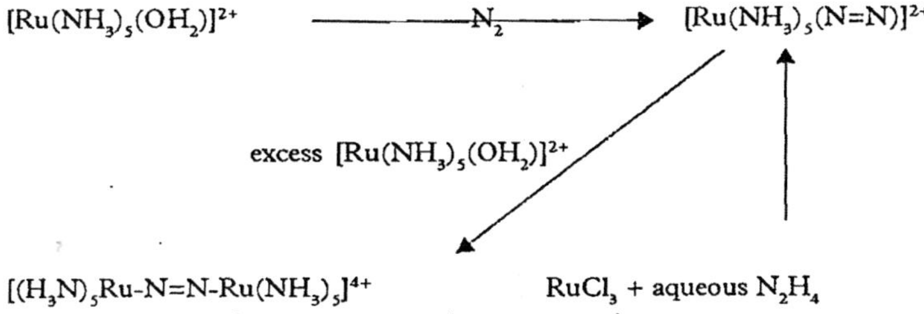


Fig. 14.5: Synthesis of a dinitrogen complexes.

Dinitrogen complexes have a very real importance. It has been recognised for some time that a class of metalloenzymes known as nitrogenases catalyse the reduction of $N_2$ to ammonia under ambient conditions in aqueous media. This would be a very valuable process if one could accomplish this on an industrial scale under mild conditions. The biological process involves bacteria in the root nodules of plants such as clover and is molybdenum based, (molybdenum is the only second row *d*-block element demonstrated to have a role as a necessary trace element).

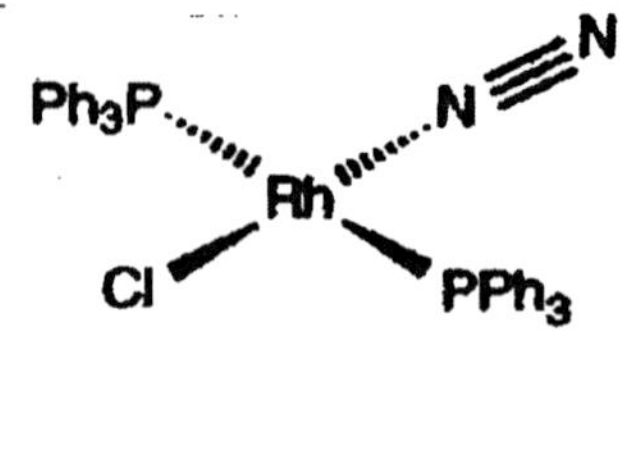


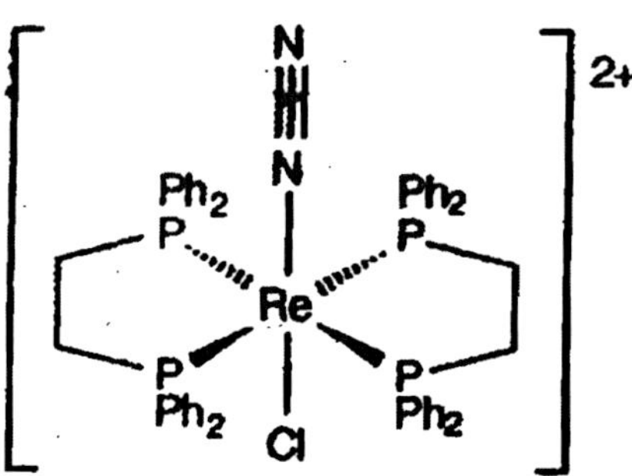


Fig. 14.6: Other examples of metal dinitrogen complexes.

A few examples are known in which dinitrogen is converted into ammonia from relatively simple dinitrogen complexes (Fig. 14.7). The interesting thing about this dinitrogen complex is that treatment with acid causes evolution of ammonia, effectively a nitrogen fixation. Experiments such as this are interesting as they might be 'model systems' for the biological fixation of nitrogen.

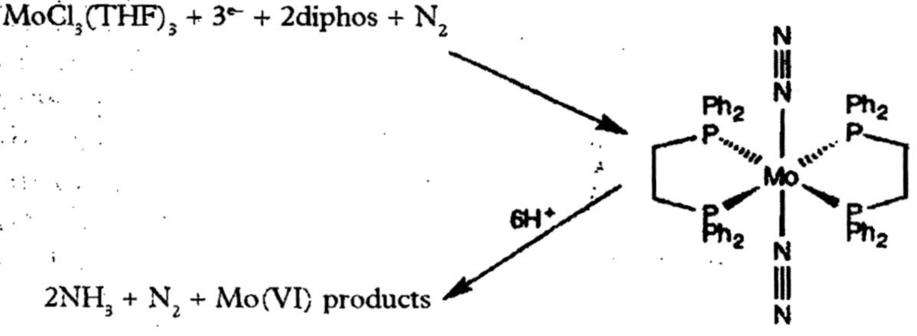


Fig. 14.7. Formation of $NH_3$ in the laboratory

# 15

# METAL NITROSYLS

## Introduction

The nitrosonium ion, $NO^+$, is isoelectronic with CO. It is therefore perhaps not surprising that there are many complexes of $NO^+$ (nitrosyl) that are both isoelectronic and isostructural with carbonyl complexes. For the purpose of the oxidation state formalism, the ligand is regarded as $NO^+$ ($:N{=}O^+$) since this leaves both atoms with an octet of electrons. This leads to very low *formal* oxidation states (some examples of oxidation state determinations are shown is Table 15.1) but recall again that oxidation state is a formalism and does not have any relation to the actual charge on the metal. In metal nitrosyl complexes the M—N distance is *shorter* than the sum of the covalent radii of the metal and nitrogen, indicating some back-bonding.

The importance of nitrosyls is partly to do with atmospheric nitrogen oxides. They are harmful and enter the environment through, for instance, car exhausts. This will no doubt lead to further interest in their chemistry. Ruthenium in particular seems to have a marked affinity for nitrosyls and this is one of the reasons why it is incorporated into catalytic converters.

There is a complication for nitrosyl complexes. In some complexes (Fig. 15.1), the nitrosyl group bonds in a quite different fashion. The alternative geometry has a *bent* M—N—O interaction.

Typical values for the M—N—O bond angle in such cases are 120—140°. This is a *distinct structural difference* from the more usual linear nitrosyls and does not arise from solid state packing effects. For oxidation state formalism purposes a bent nitrosyl is regarded as a complex of $NO^-$ (:$N^-$=O, again both atoms are in octet configurations).

Figure 15.2 shows the formal derivation of linear and bent nitrosyls from neutral NO and indicates the oxidation state conventions for NO ligands. Formally, the transformation of a linear nitrosyl into a bent nitrosyl is an internal transfer of a pair of electrons from the metal, (oxidation by 2 units) to the $NO^+$ ligand, which is reduced by two units, making it $NO^-$. The nitrogen rehybridizes to $sp^2$ , making the M—N—O bond bent.

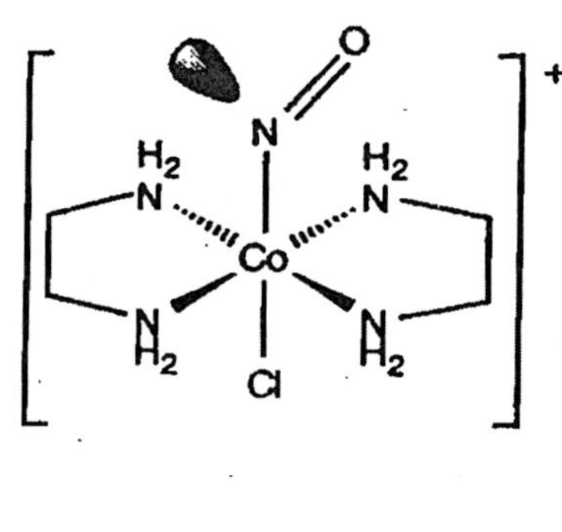


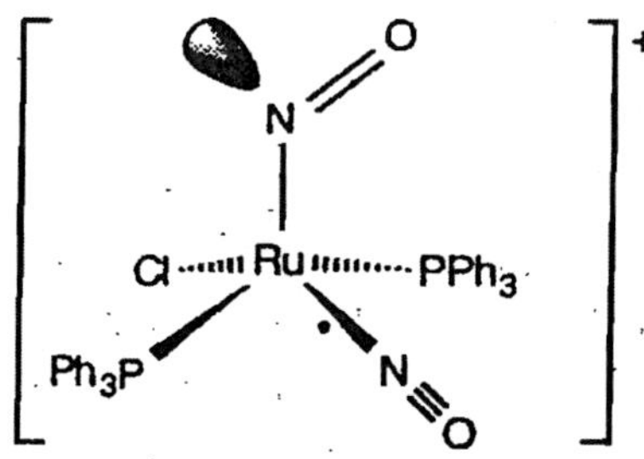


Fig. 15.1: Examples of bent nitrosyl complexes.

Table 15.1
**Examples of Oxidation State Determinations for Nitrosyl Complexes.**

| *$[Cr(NO)_4]$* | *contribution* | *running total* |
|---|---|---|
| number of Cr(O) valence electrons | 6 | 6 |
| charge on complex: 0, assume metal centred, | 0 | 6 |
| remove four $NO^+$ ligands, therefore add 4 | 4 | 10 |
| difference between 6 and 10 gives oxidation state | | -4 |

| *$[Mn(CO)_3(NO)]$* | *contribution* | *running total* |
|---|---|---|
| number of Mn(O) valence electrons | 7 | 7 |
| charge on complex: 0, assume metal centred, | 0 | 7 |
| remove three neutral CO ligands | 0 | 7 |
| remove one $NO^+$ ligand, therefore add 1 | 0 | 7 |
| difference between 7 and 8 gives oxidation state | | -1 |

| *$[RuCl(PPh_3)_2(NO)_2]^+$ (Fig. 15.1)* | *contribution* | *running total* |
|---|---|---|
| number of Ru(O) valence electrons | 8 | 8 |
| charge on complex: +1, assume metal centred, | -1 | 7 |
| remove one anionic $Cl^-$ ligand, therefore subtract 1 | -1 | 6 |
| remove two neutral $PPh_3$ ligands | 0 | 6 |
| remove one $NO^+$ ligand, therefore add 1 | 1 | 7 |
| remove one $NO^-$ ligand, therefore subtract 1 | -1 | 6 |
| difference between 8 and 6 gives oxidation state | | 2 |

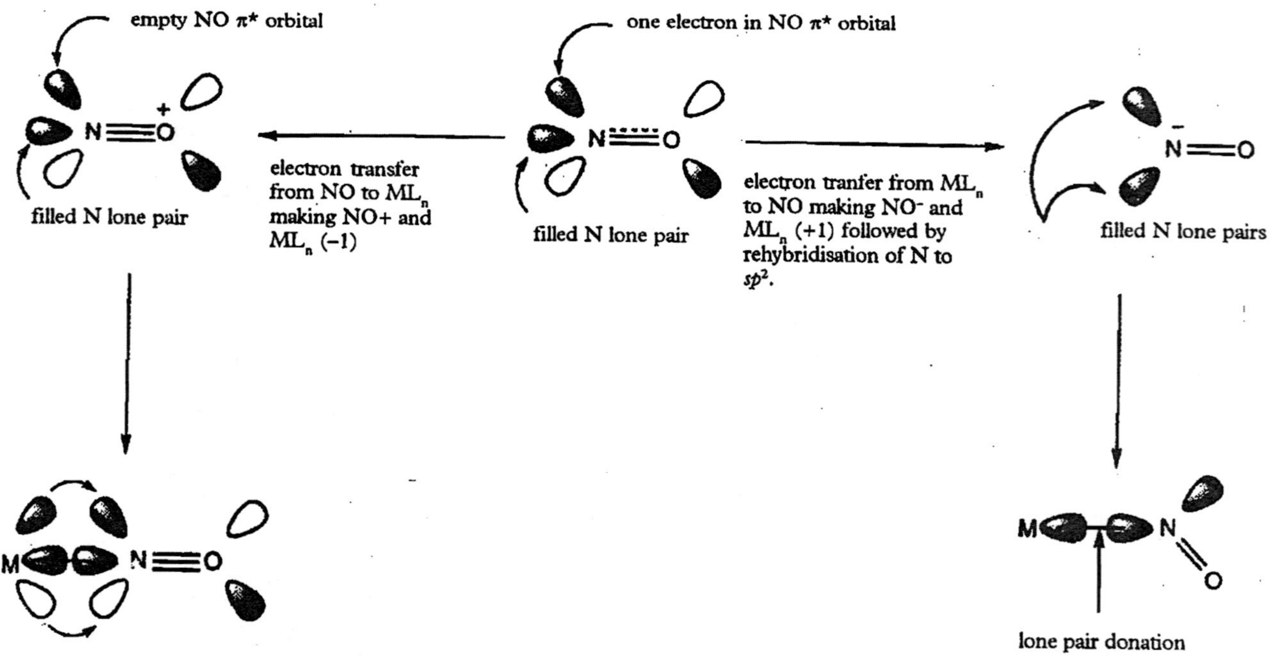


Fig. 15.2: The formal relationship between bent (complex of $NO^-$) and linear (complex of $NO^+$) nitrosyl complexes.

# 16

# KINETICS AND MECHANISMS OF REACTIONS

## Introduction

The sign of $\Delta G^{\circ}$ for a reaction is an indication of its feasibility. A negative value of $\Delta G^{\circ}$ indicates that the position of equilibrium favours the products. Although that criterion may be fulfilled there are *kinetic barriers* which may cause a reaction to be extremely slow. This section is resticted to an account of ligand substitution reactions. Redox reactions and their mechanisms are dealt with in the succeeding section.

## Ligand Substitution Reactions

There are three classes of ligand substitution reactions:

(i) *Associative* (A) reactions in which the rate determining step is that which involves the association of the two reactants - the complex and the incoming ligand. The first stage of the reaction is the production of an intermediate (not a transition state) where the metal centre has a coordination number one more than it has in the initial state.

(ii) *Interchange* (I) reactions which are single stage processes not involving an intermediate of any kind. In this kind of process, there is a synchronous interchange so that, as the incoming ligand approaches the complex, the outgoing ligand leaves. It has been necessary to define two sub-sections of interchange reactions. One is the $I_a$ process in which the rate depends upon the nature of the incoming group as well as its concentration. In such a case, bond formation in the transition state is important in determining the magnitude of the activation energy. The other sub-section consists of $I_d$ processes in which the rate is independent of the nature of the incoming group but may depend upon its concentration. The activation evergy is largely determined by bond breaking in the transition state. In such a process the incoming ligand enters the outer sphere of the complex as the leaving group dissociates (hence $I_d$) from the central atom.

(iii) *Dissociative* (D) reactions in which there is a detectable intermediate with a coordination number which is lower than that of the reactant complex.

The above classification derives from the ideas of Langford and Gray. and is in general use in this branch of kinetic investigation.

Only two general examples of ligand substitution reactions are dealt with in this book; (i) square planar platinum (II) complexes and (ii) octahedral complexes.

## Ligand Substitution Reactions of Platinum (II) Complexes

Platinum(II) complexes are in genreal square planar and conform to the associative interchange ($I_a$) mechanism. The incoming ligand is able to approach the complex without experiencing much steric hindrance. There are complications with the participation of the solvent. The observed rate laws for such reactions as:

$$PtL_3X + Y \rightarrow PtL_3Y + X$$

in which X represents the outgoing ligand, L represents ligands which remain attached to the metal centre (spectator ligands) and Y is the incoming ligand, have the form:

$$\text{Rate} = K_{obs}\,[PtL_3X] \qquad (1)$$

This is the case where the reactions are carried out under *pseudo-first order* conditions with an excess of Y (compared to the concentration of the platinum complex). Under such conditions the change in the concentration of Y is minimal and [Y] can be regarded as a constant term. The observed pseudo-first order rate constant, $k_{obs,}$ is found (by carrying out reactions with diferent concentrations of Y) to have the form:

$$k_{obs} = k_s + k_y[Y] \qquad (2)$$

in which $k_S$ and $k_Y$ are rate constants. Whenever the observed rate constant has a form such as this the interpretation is that there must be two competing pathways for the observed reaction. The expression for $K_{obs,}$ equation (2), may be placed into equation (1) and then multiplied out to give:

$$\text{Rate} = (k_S + k_Y [Y])[PtL_3X] = k_S [PtL_3X] + k_Y [Y][PtL_3X] \qquad (3)$$

the two terms representing the rates of the competing pathways. The second term is that which would be expected for a simple bimolecular association between the two reactants. The first term is independent of the concentration of the incoming ligand and may be thought to be typical of a dissociative process. When experiments are carried out with different solvents it becomes clear that the first term represents a pathway in which $k_S$ is determined by the nature of the solvent. The rate determining step does not involve the incoming ligand and is a slow process in which X is possibly replaced by a solvent molecule, S:

$$PtL_3X + S \rightarrow PtL_3S + X$$

the solvent molecule being itself replaced by a faster (and therefore not rate limiting) step:

$$PtL_3S + Y \rightarrow PtL_3Y + S$$

## Ligand Substitution Reactions of Octahedral Complexes

The discussion of these reactions is limited to the replacement of coordinated water molecules by water molecules (exchange reactions) or by other ligands. The mechanism of reactions of six coordinate complexes is dominated by the dissociative (D) or dissociative interchange ($I_d$) processes. It is very improbable that an associative process with the production of a seven coordinate intermediate (or transition state) would be able to compete with the dissociative alternatives.

An important possibility in these reactions is the formation of an outer-sphere complex between the six coordinate complex and the incoming ligand:

$$ML_5X + Y \rightarrow ML_5X,Y$$

in which the incoming ligand, Y, replaces one of the water molecules in the outer sphere or solvation shell of the complex, $ML_5X$. The second stage of the process is an $I_d$ type of ligand substitution between the inner sphere and outer sphere:

$$ML_5X,Y \rightarrow ML_5Y,X$$

The outgoing ligand, X, then equilibrates with the bulk solution phase, thus completing the substitution reaction.

$$ML_5Y,X + H_2O \rightarrow ML_5Y + X$$

If an equilibrium is established between the complex, C $(=ML_5X)$, and the incoming ligand, Y, to give an outer sphere complex, OS:

$$C + Y \rightleftharpoons OS \qquad (4)$$

the equilibrium constant, $K_{OS,}$ is given by:

$$K_{OS} = \frac{[OS]}{[C][Y]} \qquad (5)$$

If the rate determining step is the interchange reaction, the rate will be first order in [OS]:

$$\text{Rate} = K_1[OS] \qquad (6)$$

where $k_1$ is the rate constant for the interchange reaction. Placing the expression for [OS] from equation (5) into equation (6) gives.

$$\text{Rate} = K_1K_{OS}\,[C]\,[Y] \qquad (7)$$

implying a second order process.

The total concentration of the complex undergoing substitution, *T*, is given by:

$$T = [C] + [OS]$$
$$= [C] + K_{OS}\,[C]\,[Y] \qquad (8)$$

and solving this equation for [C] gives:

$$[C] = \frac{T}{1 + K_{OS}[Y]} \qquad (9)$$

Substitution in equation (7) gives:

$$\text{Rate} = \frac{K_1 K_{OS} T[Y]}{(1 + K_{OS}[Y])} \qquad (10)$$

Equation (10) reduces to one implying second order Kinetics if $K_{OS}$ has a value such that $K_{OS}[Y] >> 1$ so that:

$$\text{Rate} = k_1 K_{OS} T[Y] \qquad (11)$$

(under these conditions $T \sim [C]$)

For reactions carried out under pseudo-first order conditions where $[Y] >> T$ the observed rate constants are given by:

$$K_{obs} = \frac{k_1 K_{OS}[Y]}{(1 + K_{OS}[Y])} \qquad (12)$$

which may be inverted to give:

$$\frac{1}{k_{obs}} = \frac{1}{k_1 K_{os}[Y]} + \frac{1}{k_1} \qquad (13)$$

in which form a plot of $1/k_{obs}$ against $1/[Y]$ gives a straight line with a slope of $1/k_{obs}K_{OS}$ and an intercept of $1/k_1$. Determination of the slope and intercept from experimental data gives values for both $k_1$ and $K_{OS}$.

## Rates of Water Molecule Replacement

The above formulation for the kinetics of ligand replacement reactions at an octahedral centre are modified in the case of water replacement reactions taking place in aqueous solution because of the very high concentration of the incoming ligand which is 55.5 *M*. This has the consequence that $K_{OS}[H_2O] >> 1$ so that $k_{obs} \sim k_r$.

The observed rate constants for water exchange in a series of transition metal hexaaqua-complexes are given in Table 16.1. All the aqua-complexes are of the high spin variety (water does not bond particularly strongly with +2 transition elements). There is an enormous variation in the water exchange rates of these complexes ranging from the relatively very slow $V^{II}$ to the very fast $Cr^{II}$ and $Cu^{II}$ cases.

**Table 16.1**
**Observed Rate constants for Water Exchange Reactions**

| *Central metal* | *d* | *$log(k_i/s^{-1})$* |
|---|---|---|
| $Ca^{II}$ | 0 | 8.5 |
| $V^{II}$ | 3 | 1.8 |
| $Cr^{II}$ | 4 | 9.0 |
| $Mn^{II}$ | 5 | 7.5 |
| $Fe^{II}$ | 6 | 6.5 |
| $Co^{II}$ | 7 | 6.4 |
| $Ni^{II}$ | 8 | 4.4 |
| $Cu^{II}$ | 9 | 9.0 |
| $Zn^{II}$ | 10 | 7.5 |

The reason for this variation cannot be based upon any consideration of ionic size. There is a variation of ionic radium from the largest ($Ca^{2+}$, $r_i$ = 100 pm) to the samallest ($Cu^{2+}$ $r_i$ = 57 pm) which is irrelevant compared to the variation in rate constant from the highest ($Cr^{II}$ = $Cu^{II}$, $k_i$ = $10^9$ $s^{-1}$) to the lowest ($V^{II}$, $k_i$ = 63 $s^{-1}$)-a factor of 1.58 x $10^7$. In the $Cu^{II}$ case, there is no doubt a participation of the Jahn-Teller effect which tecnds to ensure that the axial ligands are very weakly bound. In all the cases except for $Ca^{II}$ and $V^{II}$, there are $e_g$* anti-bonding electrons present which weaken the metal-ligand binding and in the $V^{II}$ case the symmetrical filling of the $t_{2g}$ orbitals (non-bonding) is consistent with the low rate of exchange.

The above data give rise to the classification of complexes as being either inert or labile with respect to ligand substitution. These terms belong to descriptions of kinetic behaviour and must not be confused with thermodynamic terms such as stable or unstable which are used when discussing the stability or otherwise of complexes with respect to their constituent metal and ligands.

## The Conjugate Base Mechanism of Ligand Substitution Reactions

The replacement of a chloride ion ligand by a hydroxide ion in a cobalt (III)-ammine complex:

$$Co(NH_3)_5Cl^{2+} + O^{II-} \rightarrow Co(NH_3)_5OH^{2+} + Cl^-$$

is observed to be a second-order reaction, the rate law being:

$$\text{Rate} = k_2[Co(NH_3)_5Cl^{2+}][OH^-] \qquad (14)$$

where $k_2$ is a second-order rate constant. The rate law could be interpreted in terms of an associative (A) or an associative interchange ($I_a$) process. Such processes are relatively unusual for six-coordinate complexes of cobalt(III). The expected dissociative (D) or dissociative interchange ($I_d$) processes may be assigned to reactions of ammine complexes if it is considered that they paticipate in the formation of their conjugate bases. The chloropentamminecobalt(III) ion forms its conjugate base according to the reaction:

$$Co(NH_3)_5Cl^{2+} + OH^- \rightleftharpoons Co(NH_3)_4(NH_2)Cl^+ + H_2O$$

the equilibrium constant being $K_{CB}$. The conjugate base has not been isolated and the equilibrium constant mut have a very small value. The rate determining step of the ligand substitution reaction consists of the replacement of the chloride ion ligand of the conjugate base by a hydroxide ion in a dissociative manner according to the equations:

$$Co(NH_3)_4(NH_2)Cl^+ \rightarrow Co(NH_3)_4(NH_2)^{2+} + Cl^-$$

$$Co(NH_3)_4(NH_2)^{2+} + H_2O \rightarrow Co(NH_3)_5(OH)^{2+}$$

The formation of the conjugate base reduces the overall charge on the $Co^{III}$ complex and facilitates the dissociation of the negative chloride ion. If the dissociative step is rate determining, the rate of the reaction is given by:

$$\text{Rate} = k_D[Co(NH_3)_4(NH_2)Cl^+] \qquad (15)$$

where $k_D$ is the first order dissociation rate constant. The concentration of the conjugate base is given by:

$$k_D[Co(NH_3)_4(NH_2)Cl^+] = K_{CB}[Co(NH_3)_5Cl^{2+}][OH^-] \quad (16)$$

so that equation (15) may be written in the form:

$$\text{Rate} = k_D K_{CB}[Co(NH_3)_5Cl^{2+}][OH^-] \quad (17)$$

with the product $k_D K_{CB}$ representing the second-order rate constant, $k_2$.

# 17

# KINETICS AND MECHANISMS OF REDOX PROCESSES

## Redox Reactions Between Transition Metal Complexes

There are three classes of electron transfer reactions to be discussed:

(i) one electron exchange processes between metal centres involving different oxidation states of the same metal (exchange reactions),

(ii) one electron redox processes between complexes of two different metal centres, and

(iii) redox processes involving the transfer of more than one electron.

## Exchange Reactions

The classical example of this type of process is the scrambling of the $^{55}Fe$ (radioactive, decays by electron capture with a $t_{1/2}$ of 2.73y) and $^{56}Fe$ isotopes between the (II) and (III) oxidation states:

$$^{55}Fe^{II} + {}^{56}Fe^{III} \rightarrow {}^{55}Fe^{III} + {}^{56}Fe^{II}$$

which is followed by selectively precipitating the iron (III) from solution at various times after the initial mixing of the two isotopes. The reaction is thermonetural in that $\Delta H^{\Phi}$ is zero. There is a slight entropy increase as the two isotopes become scrambled between the two oxidation states. The activation energy of the reaction is

41.4 kJ nol$^{-1}$, the bimolecular rate constant at 273 K being 0.87 L mol$^{-1}$s$^{-1}$. The rate constants of ligand water replacement in the two iron species ($Fe^{II}$, $Fe^{III}$) are $3\times10^{6}$ s$^{-1}$ and $3\times10^{3}$s$^{-1}$ respectively, which become $5.4\times10^{4}$ L mol$^{-1}$ s$^{-1}$ and 54 L mol$^{-1}$s$^{-1}$ when divided by the molarity of water (55.5*M*) to convert them into bimolecular rate constants. Both those rate constants are far greater than that observed for the exchange process and this precludes the so-called inner sphere mechanism in which one ion loses a ligand by dissociation and a bridged complex is formed with the other ion which facilitates electron transfer. The $Fe^{II}$, $Fe^{II}$ exchange reaction takes place by the outer sphere mechanism is which both reactant complexes retain their inner coordination spheres.

Another factor which would rule out the formation of a bridged intermediate complex is that the water molecule has only one pair of non-bonding electrons of high enough energy to participate in bonding to a metal centre. There are two main factors which cause the reaction to have a reasonably high activation energy. These are (i) the overcoming of the electrostatic repulsion between the two ions, and (ii) the 'Franck-Condon' restriction which permits electron transfer only when the two ions have identical Fe-O distances. The Franck-Condon Principle is important in electronic spectroscopy and indicates that 'the vertical transition between any two potential energy curves is the most probable'. It arises from the recognition that electronic transitions occur in times which are far shorter than the time for a molecular vibration to occur. Applied to exchange processes it means that, in the transition state, the metal-ligand distances must be identical for the two participants, otherwise the first law of thermodynamics would be violated! The ground state ions would, if an electron were to be transferred, become vibrationally excited states which could relax to their respective ground states with the production of energy. The smaller $Fe^{III}$-O bonds must therefore be stretched and the larger $Fe^{II}$-O bonds must contract (both by vibrational excitation) before the electron may be transferred.

The mechanism whereby the two ions approach each other so that their primary solvation shells are within appropriate Van der Waals radii is known as the *outer sphere mechanism.* In this mechanism, the inner spheres (the primary coordination spheres) of the two reactants remain intact throughout the process.

The most convincing evidence which supports the outer sphere mechanism is for the reaction:

$$Fe(CH)_6^{4-} + Fe(phen)_3^{3+} \rightarrow Fe(CN)_6^{3-} + Fe(phen)_3^{2+}$$

which has a very high rate of exchange. All four participating complexes undergo ligand hydrolysis at very low rates. The inner sphere mechanism is thus precluded. The rate constants for isotopic scrambling in the couples: $Fe(CN)_6^{3-}$ + $Fe(CN)_6^{4-}$ and $Fe(phen)_3^{3+}/Fe(phen)_3^{2+}$ are $3 \times 10^2$ and > $10^5$ L $mol^{-1}$ $s^{-1}$ respectively, again indicating that the outer sphere mechanism must apply.

## One-Electron Redox Processes

When one electron is transferred between oxidation states of different elements there is no Frank-Condon restriction in operation. The mechanism of any one process may be either outer sphere or inner sphere. The classical work of H. Taube (Nobel prize winner for Chemistry, 1983) established the criteria for the operation of the *inner sphere mechanism.*

The reaction:

$$Cr(H_2O)_6^{2+} + Co(NH_3)_5Cl^{2+} + 5H_3O^+ \rightarrow Cr(H_2O)_5Cl^{2+} + Co(H_2O)_6^{2+} + 5NH_4^+$$

has a rate constant of $6 \times 10^5$ L $mol^{-1}s^{-1}$ at 298K. The $Cr^{II}$ reactant has $d^4$ configuration and is expected to be substitutionally labile, the rate constant for water exchange being $10^9$ $s^{-1}$. The cobalt(III) complex has a $d^6$ configuration and is thus substitutionally inert and has a hydrolysis rate constant of $1.7 \times 10^{-7}$ $s^{-1}$. The mechanism of the above reaction is thought to involve the replacement of a water ligand of the $Cr^{II}$ complex by the chloride ion ligand of the $Co^{III}$ complex to form a *bridged activated complex* in which the electron transfer may take place:

$$Cr(H_2O)_6^{2+} \rightarrow Cr(H_2O)_5^{2+} + H_2O$$

$Cr(H_2O)_5^{2+} + Co(NH_3)_5Cl^{2+} \rightarrow (H_2O)_5Cr^{II}ClCo^{III}(NH_3)_5^{4+} \leftrightarrow$
$(H_2O)_5Cr^{III}ClCo^{II}(NH_3)_5^{4+}$

Both formulations of the bridged activated complex contribute to the transition state and when in the right hand form there is a dissociation such that the chloride ion is retained by the $Cr^{III}$ (the $d^3$ configuration causing substitutional inertness), the other product is (initially) the substitutionally labile, $d^7$, $Co^{II}(NH_3)_5^{2+}$ ion which loses all five of its ammonia ligands to the bulk solution with the addition of six water ligands. There is no other way in which the chloride ion could be transferred between the $Cr^{II}$ and $Co^{III}$ complexes. If the $Co^{III}$ complex released the chloride ion into the bulk solution (which is a very slow process) the labile $Cr^{II}$ complex would not be likely to react with it. If an electron were to be transferred by an outer sphere process then the chloride would appear in the bulk solution (released by the labile $Co^{II}$ and would be unable to react with the inert $Cr^{III}$ which would appear as the hexaaquo-complex). Confirmatory evidence for the inner sphere mechanism is furnished by the observation that if the reaction is carried out in the presence of free $^{36}Cl^-$ (Radioactive, $t_{½} = 3.01\times10^5$ y, $b^-$ and $b^+$ emissions) there is no incorporation of the radioactive chloride ion by the $Cr^{III}$ product.

It should be noted that the chloride ion does possess a suitable pair of non-bonding electrons which allows it to act as a bridging ligand. The reaction of $[Co(NH_3)_6]^{3+}$ with $[Cr(H_2O)_3]^{2+}$ is a very slow process, with a rate constant of $10^{-3}$ L $mol^{-1}$ $s^{-1}$- a factor of $6\times10^8$ times slower than the reaction involving a chloride ligand, the ammonia molecule being unable to participate in bridge formation. The mechanism must be of an outer sphere type.

## Multiple Electron Redox Reactions

The basic rule for so-called *non-complementary* reactions in which the changes in oxidation state of the oxidising and reducing agents are different is that the mechanism will consist of the smallest number of one-electron steps. In the reaction:

$$Cr^{VI} + 3Fe^{II} \rightarrow Cr^{III} + 3Fe^{III}$$

the observed rate law for the production of $Cr^{II}$ is:

$$\frac{d[Cr^{III}]}{dt} = \frac{k[Cr^{VI}][Fe^{II}]^2}{1+\left(\frac{k'[Fe^{II}]}{[Fe^{III}}\right)} \quad (1)$$

where $k$ and $k'$ are rate constants.

This may be explained by the three one-electron steps:

$Cr^{VI} + Fe^{II} \rightarrow Cr^{V} + Fe^{III}$ (Rate constant = $k_1$) (2)

$Cr^{V} + Fe^{II} \rightarrow Cr^{IV} + Fe^{III}$ (Rate constant = $k_2$) (3)

$Cr^{IV} + Fe^{II} \rightarrow Cr^{III} + Fe^{III}$ (Rate constant=$k_3$) (4)

with the reverse of reaction (2) being important (rate constant given by $k_{-1}$). The mechanism involves two reactive intermediates—$Cr^{V}$ and $Cr^{IV}$—whose respective concentrations would attain steady state values consistent with the equations:

$$d[Cr^{V}]/dt = k_1[Cr^{VI}][Fe^{II}]-k_{-1}[Cr^{V}][Fe^{III}]-k_2[Cr^{V}]Fe^{II}] = 0 \quad (5)$$

and

$$d[Cr^{IV}]/dt = k_2[Cr^{V}]Fe^{II}] - k_3[Cr^{IV}][Fe^{II}] = 0 \quad (6)$$

*Digression on Steady State Theory*

It is a normal practice, when dealing with reaction mechanisms, to assume that there is a *rate-determining step* which is the slowest reaction in the sequence. Other steps in the mechanism are assumed to proceed at higher rates and the overall rates of production and reaction of reactive intermediates (these are identifiable species, not to be confused with transition states) are assumed to be equal, so leading to a steady state concentrations of the intermediates. The steady state assumption can be written as :

$$\frac{d[\text{reactive int ermediate }]}{dt} = 0 \quad (7)$$

The equation for the rate of production of $Cr^{III}$ —the final chromium product—is:

$$d[Cr^{III}]/dt = k_3[Cr^{IV}][Fe^{II}] = k_2[Cr^{V}][Fe^{II}] \quad (8)$$

and the unknown $[Cr^{V}]$ may be derived from equation (5):

$$[Cr^{V}] = \frac{k_1[Cr^{VI}][Fe^{II}]}{k_{-1}[Fe^{III}] + k_2[Fe^{II}]} \quad (9)$$

the final expression for the overall rate being:

$$\frac{d[Cr^{III}]}{dt} = \frac{k_1 k_2[Cr^{VI}][Fe^{II}]^2}{1+\left(\frac{k_2[Fe^{II}]}{k_{-1}[Fe^{III}]}\right)} \quad (10)$$

which is consistent with the observed rate law with $k = k_1 k_2$, and $k' = k_2/k_{-1}$.

# 18

# SPECTROCHEMICAL SERIES

## Introduction

One of the important aspects of CFT is that all ligands are not identical when it comes to causing a separation of the d-orbitals. For transition metal compounds, there is clear evidence for this from the multitude of colours available for a given metal ion when the ligands or stereochemistry are varied. In octahedral complexes, this can be considered a reflection of the energy difference between the higher $d_{z^2}$, $d_{x^2-y^2}$($e_g$ subset) and the $d_{xy}$'$d_{yz}$,$d_{xz}$ ($t_{2g}$ subset).

It has been established that the ability of ligands to cause a large splitting of the energy between the orbitals is essentially independent of the metal ion and the *Spectrochemical Series* is a list of ligands ranked in order of their ability to cause large orbital separations. Thus halides cause a small splitting and CO gives a large splitting.

## A shortened list includes:

$I^- < Br^- < SCN^- \sim Cl^- < F^- < OH^- \sim ONO^- < C_2O_4^{2-} < H_2O$

$< NCS^- < EDTA^{4-} < NH_3 \sim pyr \sim en < bupy < phen < CN^- \sim CO$

From a purely ionic basis we would expect $CO < H_2O < C_2O_4^{2-} < EDTA^{4-}$ i.e. that the most negatively charged species should interact the most strongly.

That this is not the case is a reflection of covalent interactions and is a limitation of the CFT ionic model.

Ligand Field Theory can be considered an extension of Crystal Field Theory such that all levels of covalent interactions can be incorporated into the model.

Treatment of the bonding in LFT is generally done using Molecular Orbital Theory. A qualitative approach that can be used for octahedral metal complexes in given in the following 2 diagrams.

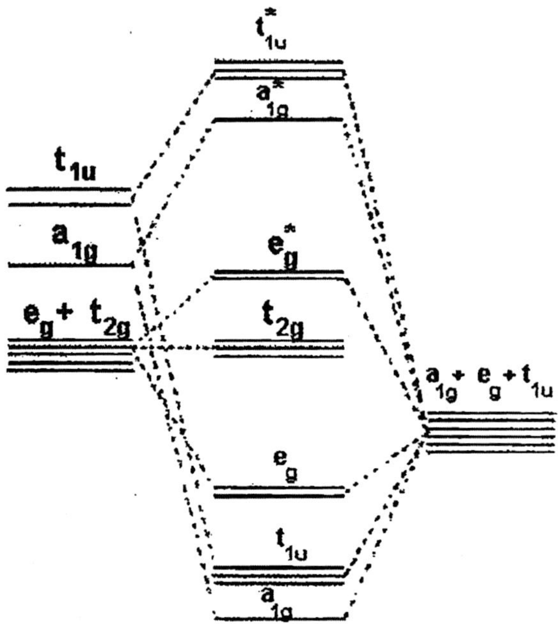


In the first diagram, only sigma bonding is considered. Orbitals derived from the metal 3d, 4s and 4p orbitals are combined with Occupied ligand group orbitals (1 from each ligand) to produce a result that shows that the metal electrons would be fed into $t_{2g}$ and eg* molecular orbitals. Note that this is similar to the CFT model except that the eg orbital is now eg*.

In the second diagram, π (pi) bonding is considered. In general π bonds are weaker than σ (sigma) bonds and so the effect is to modify rather than dramatically alter the description. 2 orbitals from each ligand are combined to give a total of 12 which are subdivided into four sets with three ligand group orbitals in each set. These are labelled $T_{1g}$, $T_{1u}$, $T_{2g}$ and $T_{2u}$. The metal $t_{2g}$ orbital is the most suitable for interaction and this is shown in the 2 cases below.

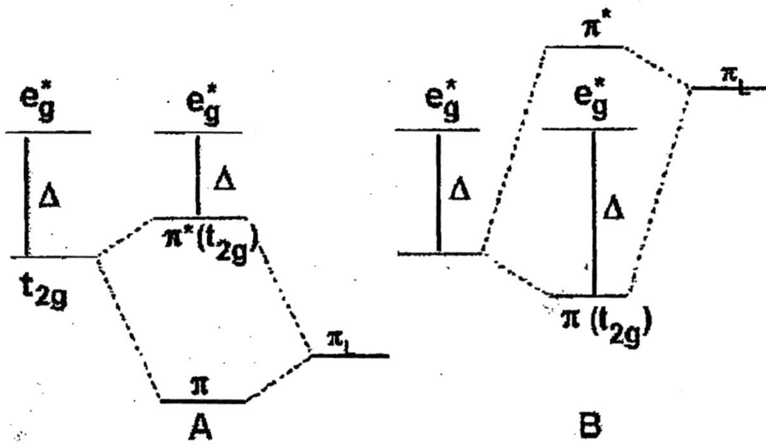


For case A, the ligand π orbitals are full and at lower energy than the metal $t_{2g}$. This causes a decrease in the sixe of Δ.

For case B, the ligand π orbitals are empty and at higher energy than the metal $t_{2g}$. This causes an increase in the size of Δ.

Returning to the problem of correctly placing ligands in the Spectrochemical series, the halides are examples of case A and groups like CN-and CO are examples of case B. It is possible then to explain the Spectrochemical series once covalent effects ar considered.

# 19

# PROBLEMS

1. Calculate the ligand field splitting parameter, $\Delta$, in $[Ni(DMF)_6]^{2+}$ given that the longest wavelength d-d bands in the spectra of $[Ni(bipy)_3]^{2+}$ and $[Ni(bipy)(DMF)_4]^{2+}$ have the wavelengths of absorption maxima at 791 nm and 985 nm respectively. Estimate $\lambda_{max}$ for the corresponding band in $[Ni(DMF)6]^{2+}$.

2. Give reasoned explanations for the following observations.

   (a) Whereas the spectrum of $[Fe(MeCN)_6]^{2+}$ has a single d-d band at 917 nm (absorption coefficient = 0.66 $m^2$ $mol^{-1}$), the spectrum of $[Fe(CN)_6]^{4-}$ has d-d bands at 270 nm and 320 nm ($\varepsilon$ = 50-350 $m^2$ $mol^{-1}$) and a much weaker band at 420 nm ($\varepsilon$ = $10^{-2}$ $m^2$ $mol^{-1}$).

   (b) The absorption spectrum of *cis*-$[Co(en)_2F_2]^+$ has bands at 360 nm and 510 nm, whereas the *trans*- isomer has weaker bands at 360, 440 and 570 nm. The spectrum of $[CoF_6]^{3-}$ has two bands at 690 nm and 877 nm.

   (c) The wavelengths, $\lambda_{max}$, of an intense band ($\epsilon$ ~200-800 $m^2$ $mol^{-1}$)of the following complex anions are:

| Complex | $[RuCl_6]^{3-}$ | $[RuCl_6]^{2-}$ | $[OsCl_6]^{2-}$ | $[OsI_6]^{2-}$ |
|---|---|---|---|---|
| $\lambda_{max}$/nm | 309 | 406 | 383 | 537 |

   (d) The molar absorption coefficients, $\epsilon$, of the sharp visible bands of $[Mn(H_2O)_6]^{2+}$ lie in the range 0.002-0.004 $m^2$

mol$^{-1}$, whereas a solution of $[Mn(H_2O_6]^{3+}$ has a very broad band at 480 nm with an ∈ value of) ~5 m$^2$ mol$^{-1}$.

(e) $[Fe(phen)_3]^{2+}$ has an absorption band at 510 nm (∈ = 1120 m$^2$ mol$^{-1}$) plus absorption bands in the UV region, whereas $[Fe(phen)_3]^{3+}$ has an absorption band at 590 nm (∈ = 100 m$^2$ mol$^{-1}$) and similar bands in the UV region.

(f) The major band in the spectrum of the pink $[Co(H_2O)_6]^{2+}$ has a maximum at 513 nm (∈ = 0.5 m$^2$ mol$^{-1}$). On the addition of HCl (conc.) the solution turns blue and is more intensely coloured with absorption maxima at 625, 670 and 700 nm (∈~ 35 - 60 m$^2$ mol$^{-1}$).

(g) In the series $[Cr(NH_3)_6]^{3+}$, $[Cr(NH_3)_5CN]^{2+}$ and $[Cr(NH_3)_4(CN)_2]^+$ the wavelengths of the longest spin-allowed bands are 464, 451 and 437 nm respectively, whereas in the series $[Cu(NH_3)_4(H_2O)_2]^{2+}$, $[Cu(NH_3)_5(H_2O)]^{2+}$ and $[Cu(NH_3)_6]^{2+}$ the wavelengths of the only d-d band are 590, 640 and 575 nm respectively.

3. (a) On the basis of the following standard reduction potentials in acid solution, predict which species can oxidize $Fe^{II}$ to $Fe^{III}$ and which can reduce $Fe^{III}$ to $Fe^{II}$.

| Reaction | $E^{\Phi}/V$ |
|---|---|
| $Ti^{IV} + e^- \rightarrow Ti^{3+}$ | 0.01 |
| $Fe^{3+} + e^- \rightarrow Fe^{2+}$ | 0.77 |
| $Cr_2O_7^{2-} + 14H^+ + 6e^- \rightarrow 2Cr^{3+} + 7H_2O$ | 1.33 |
| $Sn^{IV} + 2e^- \rightarrow Sn^{2+}$ | 0.15 |

(b) 3.48 g of an iron oxide were dissolved in 250 cm$^3$ of dilute acid. A 25 cm$^3$ aliquot of the solution was titrated with a $Ti^{3+}$ solution (0.096 mol dm$^{-3}$) of which 31.34 cm$^3$ were required. Another 25 cm$^3$ aliquot was treated with an $Sn^{2+}$ solution sufficient to complete the reaction and the solution was them titrated with a 1/60 mol dm$^{-3}$ solution of $K_2Cr_2O_7$ of which 45.10 cm$^3$ were required. Calculate the formula of the iron oxide.

4. (a) What conclusions may be drawn from the following effective magnetic moments, μ, measured at room temperature?

| Complex | Magnetic moment, $\mu/\mu_B$ |
|---|---|
| $[(CH_3)_4N]_2[MnCl_4]$ | 5.9 |
| $K_4[Mn(CN)_6]$ | 2.2 |
| $K_2[Mn(IO_3)_6]$ | 3.82 |
| $K_3[Mn(C_2O_4)_3]$ | 4.81 |
| $K_3[Mn(CN)_5OH]$ | 2.92 |
| $[Fe(CN)_6]^{3-}$ | 2.3 |
| $[Fe(H_2O)_6]^{2+}$ | 5.3 |
| $Fe(H_2O)_6]^{3+}$ | 5.9 |
| $[FeCl_4]^{2-}$ | 5.4 |

(b) Calculate the spin-only magnetic moments for the species given below and compare them with their observed values.

| Species | $[Cr(H_2O)_6]^{3+}$ | $[Ni(H_2O)_6]^{2+}$ | $[Co\ H_2O)_6]^{2+}$ |
|---|---|---|---|
| $\mu/\mu_B$ | 3.79 | 3.27 | 5.0 |